HINDUISM AND BUDDHISM

Ananda K. Coomaraswamy

HINDUISM and BUDDHISM

NEW EDITION
REVISED AND ENLARGED
IN ACCORDANCE WITH AUTHOR'S NOTES

Edited by
KESHAVARAM N. IENGAR
and
RAMA P. COOMARASWAMY

With a Preface by
ROBERT A. STROM

INDIRA GANDHI NATIONAL CENTRE FOR THE ARTS
NEW DELHI

MANOHAR
2026

Revised edition 1999

Reprinted 2022, 2023, 2024, 2026

ISBN 978-81-7304-227-0

Published by
Indira Gandhi National Centre for the Arts
Janpath, New Delhi 110001
in association with
Ajay Kumar Jain *for*
Manohar Publishers & Distributors
4753/23 Ansari Road, Daryaganj
New Delhi 110 002

Printed at
Replika Press Pvt. Ltd.

"No learning will avail, but only being born."

—JAKOB BOEHME, *De incarnatione Verbi*, I-4-19.

"The holy/sacred writings declare everywhere that man must be emptied of himself. When thou art rid of thy-self, then art thou self-controlled, and self-controlled art self-possessed, and self-possessed possessed of God and all that He has ever made."

—MEISTER ECKHART, FRANZ PFEIFFER, p. 598.

"He who knows himself knows his Lord with a unification transcending all copartnership."

—NAJMUDDIN KUTRA (R.A. Nicholson, *Notes on Mathnawī*, I.1958-9).

"At what point will you not forget God? Whenever you do not forget yourself; for in remembering your own nothingness in regard to everything, you will also remember the transcendence of God in regard to everything."

—PHILO, *De Sacrificiis Abelis et Caini*, 5.5.

"All sacred writings that have the exploration of the Self as object declare: the annihilation of the I- postulation implies Deliverance."

—ŚRĪ RAMAṆA MAHARṢI (c. 1907), in Heinrich Zimmer, *Der Weg zum Selbst*, p. 199, 1954.

"For it behoves the mind that would be led forth and let go free to withdraw itself from the influence of everything, . . . last of all itself."

—PHILO, *Legnum Allegoriarum*, III-41.

"What is oneself ? Reason."

—MARCUS AURELIUS, *The Community with Himself*, 8.40.

CONTENTS

FOREWORD

Hinduism and Buddhism is the eleventh volume in the Indira Gandhi National Centre for the Arts (IGNCA)'s programme of re-printing Dr A.K. Coomaraswamy's Collected works, re-edited and revised.

The volume has been carefully and most meticulously edited by Keshavaram N. Iengar and Rama P. Coomaraswamy. Mr Robert A. Strom has written a Preface which condenses the method and message of A.K. Coomaraswamy succinctly. The account of reception of the book at the time of its first publication is an invaluable source for facilitating comprehension of the nature of discourse on the subject in the 1940s. IGNCA is grateful to each of them, singly and together, for preparing a revised edition after carefully taking into account A.K. Coomaraswamy's modifications and amendments. The care with which A.K. Coomaraswamy re-worked his own work bears testimony to an ever re-investigative mind. The systematic manner in which each word and phrase was re-examined and fresh references given speaks of a journey of constant self-examination. The editors, particularly Mr Iengar, has accomplished the arduous task with his usual sense of detail and precision. Sincere thanks to them.

What emerges from this volume and the illuminating Preface of Mr Strom is A.K. Coomaraswamy's deep and abiding commitment to search for essence, be it religion, philosophy or art. He moves invariably from a point of undifferentiation and oneness and then carefully traces the levels of differentiation. This is evident in all his work but particularly *Time and Eternity* and *Spiritual Authority and Temporal Power in the Indian Theory of Government.* This volume is a companion volume to the other two. His reflections on first principles are distilled here as well as his concern with notions of time and the levels of the sacerdotal and regnum in the other two.

Self-consciously eschewing the historical method (for which he was criticized by some then as he is today), A.K. Coomaraswamy plunges straight into investigating the fundamentals and not the superstructure. In the context of this not so easily definable term 'Hinduism', he stays clear of speaking of its historical origins and linear growth in terms of schools, sub-schools, cults and sects, even the discussions in the principal philosophic schools.

Instead, he clearly states his position as regards the non-acceptance of the 'historical method' and proceeds to state the fundamentals on the basis of literary source material from the *Ṛg Veda* to the Vaiṣṇava, Śaiva and Tantric theological treatises. For him, as for some other thinkers, writers and practitioners, the *Bhagavad Gītā* is probably the most important single work, which condenses the essential fundamentals in a single whole. Given this clear enunciation of his sources and position and acceptance of the centrality of the *Bhagavad Gītā*, the chapters which follow are logically divided into consideration of the myth, the theology and autology, the way of works (*karma*) and the social order.

Myth (*itihāsa*) to A.K. Coomaraswamy is 'the penultimate truth of which all experience is the temporal reflection. The mythical narrative is the timeless and place-less validity true nowhere and everywhere.' It is with this definition that he explores the myth of the endless serpent (dragon). Through carefully sifting material in the *Ṛg Veda, Kaṇvaśatapatha Brāhmaṇa,* the *Taittirīya Brāhmaṇa,* the *Muṇḍaka Upaniṣad,* he culls out the notion *tad ekam* (That One), the state without differentiation of being from non-being and the process of dismemberment and disjointedness (i.e. differentiations). The reciprocal relationship of the whole and the parts is his focus. The Dragon also the World Tree. Mountain and Cave are cognates, Coomaraswamy tells us. Although there have been considerable comments on the endless serpent and the dragon slayer, and the victim, Coomaraswamy offers a deep insight through clustering these symbols and drawing attention to the importance of the notions of exhaustion, dismemberment, swallowing and emptying and regeneration whether Dragon, Tree, Mountain or Cave. The primary meaning of Giri mountain, he reminds us, is to swallow. Each signifies the process of exhuming and being. Through the myth and its narration, A.K. Coomaraswamy focuses attention on a central principle of recognizing that there is an incessant multiplication of the inexhaustible One and unification of the indefinitely Many.

The relationship of the one and the many has indeed been a pivotal concern of whatever philosophy or religion that we today know as Hinduism. In the chapter 'Theology and Autology', he explores the relationship of the myth and the ritual (*yajña*). Through an analysis of both, he points at the second principle of conjointedness. The images of two birds on one tree or one bird with two heads do not denote contraries or binary opposites, instead conjugation (*mithunam, sambhava, eko bhava*) is a vital operation, productive of a third, which is in the image of the first and nature of the second. Thus, the conjugation of Mind (*manas*) and the Voice (*vāc*) gives birth to a concept (*saṅkalpa*). Through a series of examples, A.K. Coomaraswamy elucidates the principle of halves of the originally undivided. At the level of governance, it is sacerdotium and regnum (*brahma-kṣatrau*) the priest and the king. A.K. Coomaraswamy had unfolded clearly this relationship in *Spiritual Authority and Temporal Power in the Indian Theory of Government.* He returns to the theme to point out that at the psychological level it is the self and not-self, the inner man and outer individuality. Pertinently, he points at the tenet that the outer must submit to the inner Man. This is what is meant by insistence on self-control rather than self-assertion. Coomaraswamy concludes by saying that the theology and autology are one and the same science. The only possible answer to 'What am I?' must be 'that art Thou'. This essay like others is exemplary not only for its textual richness but for the discerning mind anxious to bring the first principles to the level of applicability in everyday active life.

In the chapter 'The Way of the Works', he facilitates a comprehension of the process of generation and division to regeneration and composition. The section on the interpretation of *bhakti* provides many much needed correctives on the origins of *bhakti.* He underscores the concept of sharing, giving God his share, as also the context of giving up your share (*bhāgam*) in the sacrifice (*yajña*). Ultimately thus the entire life of the individual is an incessant operation in each and every function of active life down to our very breathing, eating, drinking, and this operation is sacramentally interpreted. This is *karma mārga* (the way of the works) of the *Bhagavad Gītā.* It is a continual sacrifice not to be differentiated from the act of giving in the *yajña.* A.K. Coomaraswamy deduces from another moral ethical principle 'Sacrifice thus understood....'

The chapter 'The Social Order' concludes Part I relating to Hinduism. Logically, if life is a continual sacrifice, in actual practice, the method is through *yoga* (yoking together); *yogaḥ karmasu kauśalam* is the key phrase through which Coomaraswamy examines the notions of social order and its significance. This chapter needs to be carefully read by many who are today and understandably questioning and rejecting the very conception of *varna* and *āśramas.* The distortions and deformities of the original structure have been so many and so frequent that the original intent and purpose of recognizing the human at his/her most optimal in a framework of relationships spatially and temporally is all but forgotten. A.K. Coomaraswamy reminds us of the original context of the sacrifice and functional requirement of a society. The nature of this social order whether as groups or age/gender, generation was based on principles other than that of competition and conflict. In the original conception (remote and distant as it is from our historical and certainly contemporary reality), every function from that of a priest or a king down to that of a potter and scavenger, is literally a priesthood and every operation a ministerial rite. Coomaraswamy's observations provoked a controversy then as it is bound to perhaps provoke now. While little can be done to rectify the distorted and deformed structures now beyond redemption, perhaps it is still possible to re-examine the social order on the basis of recognizing and legitimatizing and giving status to all skills—cerebral, intellectual and manual alike—at their optimum and not minimum. At the level of applicability, it means the empowerment as equal status and respect of the extraordinary skilled human resources and not patronage and concessions on the basis of holding up cerebral skills as the dominant model. The implications of the rethinking would be far reaching. A.K. Coomaraswamy had questioned the advisability of adopting the industrial model for development then as some are questioning it now. Organization of societal structures and issues of empowerment on the basis of plural abilities and multiplicity of identities is a larger question not only for India or the Hindu world but for a vast majority of the erstwhile colonized world. It is time not only to reread Coomaraswamy and his interpretations but also to rethink and reflect upon our own predicament created by misinterpretation of some seminal notions as also subscription to inappropriate notions of hierarchy, function, uniformity and empowerment based on a unidimentional linear progressive model.

His comments on the *āśramas* and the gradual journey from childhood to death is also relevant. The structuring of lifespan along a certain path of acquiring experience and renunciation, allowed space for mutual respect amongst different generations. An ascending path of gradual giving up was the strategy for receiving love and respect. Here too, many lessons have to be learnt on intergeneration, gender issues which preoccupy us. Coomaraswamy deals with them with acute sensitivity.

Thus, Hinduism as elucidated by Coomaraswamy, is no historical account or a pronouncement of a religion as doctrine, faith or institution as a narrow sectarianism. It is a sincere investigation into the first principles of a world-view, a knowledge system and a social order. The myth, ritual, conduct and social order are the four dimensions and the four corners of this world-view. Each interpenetrates into the other. The one and the many, the two in one continual sacrifice (*yajña*), the yoking together (*yoga*) and webbing and interlocking are essentials at the levels of concept, thought, systems and conduct. This is a daunting challenge of perception and action before those who are now inheritors, alas also makers of a total fragmentation and chaotic dismemberment of the holistic vision distant and distorted no doubt, but still relevant.

In Part II, A.K. Coomaraswamy investigates Buddhism in a similar manner. The awakening Buddha is interpreted as a myth so as to identify the first principles and the perennial. Here also Coomaraswamy does not follow the historical path with volition. He does not consider Buddhism a heterodox development. Instead he is of the view that although Buddha did not establish a new order, he all the same restored an older form. 'I have seen' the Buddha says, 'the ancient way, the old road that was taken by the formerly, All Awakened and that is the path to follow.' He juxtaposes the Upaniṣads and the teaching of Buddha to argue that the two are closely related and concordant bodies of doctrine. Both are not opposed to each other but to a common enemy. According to A.K. Coomaraswamy, the intention of the Buddha was clearly to restore the truths in the ancient doctrine.

Çoomaraswamy restricts himself in this section to an examination of the *tripiṭaka* of *vinaya sūtra* and *abhidhamma* (monastic regimen, discourse and abstracts discourse) and does not extend his study to extra-canonical literature. In short, here also he carefully identifies his sources and his method.

Thereafter, he examines the myth and elucidates on the doctrine. Through an equally circuitous route of an examination of the texts, A.K. Coomaraswamy returns to the theme of the relation of the sacerdotium and regnum ethics and doctrine (*artha* and *dharma*). Pertinently he points out that "unselfishness from the Indian point of view is an amoral state in which no question of altruism can present itself liberation being as much from the notion of 'others' as it is from the notion of 'self'."

Equally sensitively he dwells upon the notion of 'who is awake?' The metaphor of the chariot is re-examined in Upaniṣadic and Buddhist thought to bring home essential convergence and some differences.

The Eternal Law (*dharma*) is in fact the charioteer, and the Buddha identifies himself with that self which he calls his refuge with his law and thus the best of charioteers.

And finally, A.K. Coomaraswamy concludes that there can be no doubt that Buddha—the great person *Arhat*—is himself the spirit (*ātman*) and the inner-man of all beings and that he is 'that one' who makes himself the manifold in whom all beings again become one. Buddha thus is Brahmā, Prajāpati, Light of Lights, Fire or Sun, in short the first principle, and ultimately the realization of *Nirvāṇa* is the flight of the alone to the alone and is the void that passeth to the void.

A.K. Coomaraswamy reaches out to the perennial and identifies the essence in both Hinduism and Buddhism. At a time when differentiation and assertion of narrow identities is being asserted, at the very moment of globalization at another level, the voices of the truly universal and perennial and the essential need to be heard and reflected upon. A.K. Coomaraswamy did not have a revivalist agenda as has been opined by some of his detractors and critics, it was a sincere journey towards a comprehension of the relationship of the one and the many, the you and I, thou and that.

Through these essays, he provides us the talisman with which to persevere with our respective journeys in concord and not conflict.

My renewed sincerest thanks to Rama P. Coomaraswamy, Mr K.N. Iengar and Mr Robert Strom, and my colleague Dr L.M. Gujral for making it possible to reprint the revised edition.

October 1998 KAPILA VATSYAYAN

PREFACE

"Lay hold, start up, cross over!"[1]

Hinduism and Buddhism is divided into two parts. Both main texts appear to faithfully reflect two lectures respectively titled "Hinduism" and "Buddhism" delivered on February 10 and 17 of 1942.[2] After the Philosophical Library of New York showed an interest in publishing the combined lectures, Coomaraswamy composed the notes for the book and completed his work early in 1943. The book appeared on 1 May 1943.[3] As originally published, these notes were relegated to the ends of both sections, but for this long awaited new edition, they are conveniently positioned at the bottom of the appropriate pages. We are fortunate in being able to present below a resumé of the entire opus from the author's own hand, having found and identified it among the thousands of unindexed manuscript pages and notes of Coomaraswamy. The manuscript of this page is typed and single-spaced but without title. It was intended for and in part used by the publisher for promotion probably late in 1944.[4] In our transcription, we have retained Coomaraswamy's spellings.

The two lectures, now printed with an added documentation of over 300 notes, were delivered at the Jewish Theological Seminary in New York in February 1942. The doctrines are expounded from the Indian point of view, rather than that of the Indologist whose concern is less with the Indian

[1]This exact phrase, without reference, was hand-written by Coomaraswamy at the top of the lecture manuscript of this book's "Hinduism" section. We have been able to trace it to RV.X. 53.8 and supply below Coomaraswamy's own comments as found in his "The Pilgrim's Way", JBORS, XXIII (1937), p. 466.

> . . . RV. X. 53.8 where the long sought Agni has appeared and having been called upon to "guard the pathways by contemplation wrought" and to "beget" (or) "bring forth" the Heavenly Race, addresses the *mumukṣavah* as follow: "Here flows the River of the Rock: lay hold, stand up (*ut tiṣthata*), cross over (*pratarata*), O my comrades (*sakhāyaḥ*), there let us leave behind the ineffectual (*aśēvāḥ*) and corss unto the friendly (*śivān*) coursers (*vājān*)."

We do not know when or why Coomaraswamy penned this phrase, but have found it in context to be a watchword for our work here.

[2]Letter of A.K.C. to Graham Carey, 27 April 1943. S. Durai Raja Singam, *Letters of Ananda Coomaraswamy*, Vol. 1 (1972), n.p.

[3]We have only been able to find and identify the manuscript of the "Hinduism" section, without notes, at Firestone Library, Princeton University, and believe the remaining manuscripts of the book have been lost.

[4]Only a line or two of Coomaraswamy's "Resumé" was actually used by the publisher along with a portion of the "review" by Wing-tsit Chan from 1944. See our Index of the "Reviews" below. Coomaraswamy himself preserved a copy of the "Promotion" in his desk copy of the book.

teachings than with his own interpretation of them. It is assumed, for example, that even the oldest forms of Hinduism are neither polytheistic nor pantheistic, and that no doctrine of reincarnation, other than that of the immanent God "who never became anyone", is taught. Hinduism is the oldest of the surviving mystery religions; in no fundamental sense unique, but a form of the "Wisdom uncreate" of which the formulations are essentially the same in Platonism, Christianity, Taoism and other traditional doctrines; from the Indian point of view, Agni, Buddha, Horus, Moses, Christ, and Muhammad are the varying names of the one and the same eternal avatar. There can be misunderstanding, but never a conflict of essential doctrines; for, as the Buddha says, there is but one Truth, and no other.

From the Myth as the initial and basic statement of Truth, we proceed to its ritual imitation and perpetuation in the Sacrifice, and from the formal Sacrifice to its reflection in the vocational organisation of society in which life itself is sacrificially interpreted; the object of such a society being to secure for all men, whatever their natural endowment, the means of Self-realisation. The form of such a traditional society is designed to secure at the same time temporal and eternal benefit; in art (manufacture), for example, there is no divorce of metaphysical significance from practical utility, no necessary distinction of fine from applied or sacred from profane. Man's last end is to know his real Self, not the impermanent and variable outer personality of this man so-and-so, but the Inner Man, immanent Person and immutable Self of all men alike, that can be as and when it will. "That, Brahma, immanent deity, art, thou."

The basis of Buddhism is no less mythical; the "life" of the pseudo-historical Founder, the Conqueror of Death, repeats the original myth of the archetypal dragon-slayer. His doctrine—as he asserts very forcibly—is not his own, but the opening up again of the "ancient path"; and in fact it would be difficult to discover in Buddhism anything novel, though there is much that is original. The Buddhist polemic is directed mainly against the superstition of life, against the identification of our Self with the processes of living, acting, feeling and thinking; these are useful to the wayfarer, but have no more significance when he has arrived. The Way is ethical, and involves the discrimination of what ought and ought not to be done but the goal lies beyond good and evil. Hinduism and Buddhism alike are doctrines of self-denial; whoever would save the Self, must have eradicated consciousness of self; and this is to be understood not only ethically (since where there is no "self" there is no "others") but metaphysically. The whole exposition shows that the Christian theologian who will take the trouble to study Indian religion seriously, and not merely "historically", will find in its teachings abundant "extrinsic and probable proofs" of the truth of Christian doctrine; and may at the same time, if he will abandon his "proselytising fury" realise the essential unity of all religions.

After receiving his desk copy in 1943, Coomaraswamy had it rebound with each page facing a new blank page.[5] Copious marginal addenda were added, some typed, which have made the task of the editor an essential and difficult mediation. These addenda have almost entirely been incorporated and arranged into the notes for this new edition by Mr. Iengar. One could best call the notes "foundational", but as we find in all of Coomaraswamy's late writing, they have tremendous importance and at times blossom into minor essays. The reader is urged to utilize both "upper" text and "lower" notes indivisibly: the former synthetic and far-ranging as an overview, while the latter focusing the attention on documentation and corroborative details. Few authors have ever expended as much effort as Coomaraswamy on these fine details of scholarship which are, we believe, models of academic virtue possessing intrinsic and extrinsic significance.

The reaction to the book among Coomaraswamy's friends was certainly favorable. In a letter dated 29 June 1943, Eric Schroeder, a former associate at the Museum of Fine Arts in Boston and a specialist on Persian Art, called the book "a classic, round and ripe in meaning, majestically clean in shift; and the insight which has chosen and arranged only what is eternal in these mysteries is dazzling". Marguerite Block, an editor and long-time admirer, described the work as "a distilled essence of A.K.C.".[6] Many of the published formal critiques were collected by Coomaraswamy and are preserved in his desk copy. Our index of the "Reviews", presented below as an appendix, also includes those items certainly seen by Coomaraswamy but probably only retained in the bound copies of his journals. These journals may have contained important subsidiary materials, particularly notes and comments, and were a part of the Coomaraswamy Bequest to Princeton University. They were unfortunately not preserved as a distinct body of material by the University and might even have been discarded. Our index also includes the important review of André Préau from 1948.

In reading this almost unanimous crowd of admiring witnesses, the first place must be given to René Guénon, the eminent French Traditionalist whose study on the Vedantâ should be known to many Indian savants.[7] His review, published in 1946, called *Hinduism and Buddhism* an "important ouvrage, qui rectifie un grand nombre d'erreurs et de confusions commises par les orientalistes", and unreservedly endorsed Coomaraswamy's insistence on the underlying unity of the two great spiritual currents. Dr. Murray Fowler, who was able to study under A.K.C. through an academic grant and later was associated with the University of Wisconsin (U.S.A.), clearly placed the

[5]Coomaraswamy had almost all of his late published books rebound with blank pages to allow for an easy incorporation of hand-written addendum.

[6]Letter of Margarite Block to Murray Fowler, 13 May 1943, Coomarasawamy Family Collection.

[7]Guénon, René (Trans. Richard C. Nicholson), *Man and His Becoming according to the Vedantâ*, Noonday Press, 1958. This book, which Coomaraswamy described as "probably the best account of Vedantâ in any European language" was conceived before the First World War, but not published until 1925.

Coomaraswamian "underlying unity" as a facet of a personal religious philosophy. His review from 1944 emphasized the danger of such an approach in "that the inevitable modifications imposed by local limitations of space and time upon the universal truths . . . may be overlooked, or minimized, or disregarded". However, Fowler goes on to say that this "danger" has been well noted by Coomaraswamy and that "he has not been trapped by it here". (The correlation of Indian formal terminology and their Western equivalents is specifically commended.) Fowler's qualified praise was entirely dismissed by W.E. Clark, Professor of Oriental Languages at Harvard University, in his review for the *Harvard Journal of Asiatic Studies*, August 1944. For Clark, the "danger" intimated by Fowler has overwhelmed Coomaraswamy's approach and renders the work valueless. Almost the only statement of the Clark review with which we cannot take exception is that found on p. 70: "The Buddhism and Hinduism described by Coomaraswamy are very sublimated religions which correspond to the great institutionalized religions . . . as Meister Eckhart corresponds to the great institutionalized religion of Christianity". Coomaraswamy, himself, seems to echo this remark when he summed up his perspective in the book as not "precisely" orthodox, but comparable to Thomism vis-a-vis "the notions of many ignorant Christians".[8] He would later describe the Clark review as "a real 'attack'",[9] depreciating the entire matter through the use of quotation marks.[10] A much more balanced and even-handed assessment is offered by Alban Widgery in the *Philosophical Review*. "Dr. Coomaraswamy appears to consider the fundamental [doctrine] of the *Philosophia Perennis* [i.e. the transcendent Unity of the various metaphysical dialects of humanity], to be essentially . . . the Advaitist . . . Vedantic doctrine." Also the anonymous author of the review in the *Jour. of Bible and Religion* helps to define the parameters of these academic "clashing opposites" where he writes "the author does not use the historical method. Unlike such Indianists as Lionel Barnett, Nocol Macnicol and De la Vallee-Poussin he does not trace stages in development of doctrine. Instead he follows the orthodox Indian technique of detecting timeless truths through meditation over many texts until affirmations rise which can be checked closely by authority. Lifelong study of Sanskrit and Pali texts enables him to carry through this method effectively and with ripe erudition. For the historically-minded student this is seen to involve a certain backward reading into primitive texts of profound ideas [only] developed later. From the angle of Coomaraswmy's approach, however, that does not matter for the revelation (*sruti*) is already present in

[8]Letter of A.K.C. to Ade Bethune, 1 July 1943. S. Durai Raja Singam, *Letters*, Vol. 4 (1974), n.p.

[9]Letter of A.K.C. to Jean-Albert Cuttat, 29 July 1944, Coomarsawamy Family Collection.

[10]We should like to mention in addition that Coomaraswamy left a short hand-written note among the end-papers of his desk copy in which he directed the reader to his revised note 47 (Buddhism) at the beginning of the chapter "The Doctrine" in the "Buddhism" section of the book for a "rebuttal" of Clark.

the picturings of primitive myth . . . this work definitely sets aside the historical approach with its many questions of chronology and development, criticism from that angle is gratuitous." It is ironic that Clark called one of the Coomaraswamy's instances for the a-temporal and eternal Tradition a "gratuitous assumption".[11]

We have found that the contesting schools of historicism and idealism, represented in the official reaction to *Hinduism and Buddhism*, are merely another name for one of the book's main themes: the eternal battle of soul and Spirit. This was a major leitmotif in all of Coomaraswamy's late oeuvre, examined ontologically in terms of the inherent duality within creation or manifestation, the anthropological and psychological essays use it to define the nature of the human microcosm, while the social, political, and polemical essays use it to define the "Devil's playground" or the Dragon "Holdfast" who will not set "God's people free". Coomaraswamy's profound awareness of the causes of the conflict within ourselves and between societies, the "war" among our many selves, also and inversely allowed him to rise above the fray. It is in that "moment" (really timeless) and where all possible Ways become One that we hear the voice of the God:

> Indestructible,
> Learn thou! the Life is, spreading life through;
> It cannot anywhere, by any means,
> Be anywise diminished, stayed, or changed.
> But for these fleeting frames which it informs
> With Spirit deathless, endless, infinite,
> They perish. Let them perish, Prince! and fight! . . .
> Life cannot slay. Life is not slain!

Bhagavad Gītā 2

> . . . thou . . . be free of the "pairs of opposites", and free
> From that sad righteousness which calculates; . . .

Bhagavad Gītā 3[12]

We see from this that it is a duty imposed by our state to "fight". Just as much, it is the duty of the accomplished to find in faith the assurance of final victory. Only a warrior for *Dharma*[13] like Coomaraswamy can show the Way to the Primordial Unity, and win the Kingdom of Heaven through "violence". thereby reversing time, or renewing time, and like the action and reaction of clapper and bell or stone against striking stone engender once again the

[11]See p. 66 of the Clark review in the HJAS and our Index of the reviews for the exact reference.

[12]Sir Edwin Arnold, Trans., *Bhagavad Gita/ The Song Celestial*, Heritage Press, 1961, pp. 9, 17.

[13]S. Durai Raja Singam called Coomaraswamy a "Warrior for *Dharma*" in one of his many useful encomiums.

primordial *son et lumiere*—both music of the spheres, *Logos* and "Light of the World". A "position" actually unstable and unreal which fails to comprehend and address the inevitable simplifications and telescoping of the synthetic "approach" is finally itself lost in the unreality of an insistent, unblinking categorization. Finally, those who cannot or will not escape from their local coloring (and what a "bleaching" takes the manifest being to be entirely free from heredity and genetic "shading") and make the profound, inevitable descent (ascent)[14] into the ground of Being (Non-Being) can hope to understand any-thing—that is, grasp relationships and even begin to think. What shocks the historicist in this book is the active immutable reign of the Spirit wherever that has been manifested from the heart of the sanctioned Traditions. In India, this has lately been the province of Advaita Vedantâ, with which Coomaraswamy explicitly identified himself.[15] While we are in this world, we are inevitably brought to make a judgment in which sides are "weighed" and where "weight" is always found wanting. But if one sifts the matter with the wisdom of a Coomaraswamy what will appear on the narrow stage of the circumscribed to be irreconcilable is well-known brotherly love in the "Green Room".[16] We can be confident that it was from such a "Tiring Room" as this that Coomaraswamy calmly took up the cudgels of his polemic and it was to such a benign room that he retired when *his* time was up.

INDEX TO REVIEWS

(Author not given), *Garrett (Mass.) Tower*, November 1943 (no pagination available). A.K.C.'s desk copy.

(Author not given), *Journal of Bible and Religion* 13, No. 2, May 1945, pp. 115-16. A.K.C.'s desk copy.

(Author not given), *Mind Digest*, Feb. 1946 (no pagination available). A.K.C.'s desk copy.

Chan, Wing-tsit, *Phil. Abs.* 13-14 (1944), p. 6. A.K.C.'s desk copy. A portion of this review was used in the publisher's "promotion".

Clark, Walter E., *Harvard J. As. S.*, Aug. 1944, pp. 63-70. Known to A.K.C.

Das, Taraknath, *Asia and the Americas*, Nov. 1943 (no pagination available). A.K.C.'s desk copy.

R.T.F., *Personalist* (n.d. or pagination). A.K.C.'s desk copy.

Fowler, Murray, *Review of Religion* VIII (1944), No. 3, pp. 281-4.

[14]The many possible ways are finally One Way.

[15]Coomaraswamy called himself a "Vedantist" in an unpublished portion of his lecture "The Indian Doctrine of Man's Last End", which we have recently edited and hope to see appear in the journal *Sophia*, Oakton, VA (U.S.A.).

[16]The 'Green Room' was the subject of no specific work by Coomaraswamy but seems to figure prominently in his consciousness, especially in such works as the "Khwaja Khadir and the Fountain of Life . . .", 1934, and "Sir Gawain and the Green Knight", 1944, to only name the most obvious choices.

Guénon, René, *Études Traditionelles*, Aug. 1946, pp. 337ff. Not in A.K.C.'s desk copy but we have examined A.K.C.'s bound copy of this journal. See also the short notice by Guénon in *E.T.*, 1951, p. 94.

Gulick, Sidney, "Oriental Conceptions of the Self", *Personalist* XXVII (1946), pp. 306-13. Not in A.K.C.'s desk copy and possibly not known to Coomaraswamy though he and Gulick did exchange a number of letters.

(P.H.), *Freedom* (n.d. or pagination available). A.K.C.'s desk copy.

Hiriyana, M., *Aryan Path*, Feb. 1944, pp. 76-7. A.K.C.'s desk copy.

Hollis, Howard, *J.A.A.C.*, 1943, pp. 89-91. Not collectd by A.K.C. but almost certainly known to him.

(K.P.L.), *Jour. Phil.* XL (1943), pp. 723-4. A.K.C.'s desk copy.

Préau, André, "A.K. Coomaraswamy et la Pense de l'Inde", *Cahiers du Sud* 290 (1948), pp. 126-32. Not collected by A.K.C. See also Preau's review in *Cahiers du Sud*, 1951, pp. 166-8 on the appearance of the French translation by René Allar and Pierre Ponsoye (1950, Gallimard).

Rind, George C., *Modern Schoolman* XX (n.d. or pagination available). A.K.C.'s desk copy.

Scherman, Lucian, "Indische Weisheit", JAOS LXIII (1943), pp. 241-62. Not in A.K.C.'s desk copy, but certainly known to him.

Stigall, John, *Far Eastern Survey*, 22 Sep. 1943 (no pagination available). A.K.C.'s desk copy.

Tyberg, Judith, "Hinduism and Buddhism", *Theosophical Review*, March 1944, pp. 123-5. A.K.C.'s desk copy.

Varadachari, K.C., *Hindu*, Madras, 23 Jan. 1944 (no pagination available). A.K.C.'s desk copy.

(F.C.W), *The Standard*, 1943 (no pagination available). A.K.C.'s desk copy.

Wach, Joachim, *Journal of Religion*, Jan. 1946 p. 60. A.K.C.'s desk copy.

Widgery, Alban G., *Philosophical Review* LIII (1944), pp. 605-7. A.K.C.'s desk copy.

ACKNOWLEDGEMENTS

It would be impossible to list the names of all the individuals who have in one way or another contributed to this second edition of *Hinduism and Buddhism*. However, thanks must be rendered to some of the individuals involved. I would first of all like to express my gratitude to Dr. Kapila Vatsyayan whose encouragement and suggestions have made possible the republication of this and many other works of Dr. Ananda K. Coomaraswamy; and to Dr. Lalit Gujral whose continued efforts have guided the text through the hands of editors and publishers. I am grateful to Mrs. Regeen Najar of New York City who holds the copyright to the first edition and who has cooperated and encouraged the editing and publishing of this second edition. Of the many scholars who have assisted in identifying and translating references, special mention should be made of Robert Strom (the author of the Preface), Dr. Wolfgang Smith, Alvin Moore Jr., Mr. Eric Hansen and Mrs. Marie Hansen.

Particular thanks must be given to Mr. K. Ienger who did the major part of the editing and whose knowledge of Sanskrit and the original texts has been most important.

RAMA P. COOMARASWAMY

HINDUISM

INTRODUCTION

Brahmanism or Hinduism[*] is not only the oldest of the mystery religions, or rather metaphysical disciplines, of which we have a full and precise knowledge from literary sources, and as regards the last two thousand years also from iconographic documents, but also perhaps the only one of these that has survived with an unbroken tradition and that is lived and understood at the present day by many millions of men, of whom some are peasants and others learned men well able to explain their faith in European as well as in their own languages. Nevertheless, and although the ancient and modern scriptures and practices of Hinduism have been examined by European scholars for more than a century, it would be hardly an exaggeration to say that a faithful account of Hinduism might well be given in the form of a categorical denial of most of the statements that have been made about it by European scholars and by Indians trained in our modern sceptical and evolutionary modes of thought.[1]

One would begin, for example, by remarking that the Vedic doctrine is neither pantheistic[2] nor polytheistic, nor a worship of the powers of Nature except in the sense that *Natura naturans est Deus* and all her powers but the names of God's acts; that *karma* is not "fate" except in the orthodox sense of the character and destiny that inhere in created things themselves, and rightly understood, determines their vocation;[3] that *māyā* is not "illusion", but rather the maternal measure and means essential to the manifestation of a quantitative and in this sense "material", world of appearances, by which we may be either enlightened or deluded according to the degree of our own maturity; that the notion of a "reincarnation" in the popular sense of the

[*]The term Brahminism to designate the religion of the Hindus was erroneously applied first by the Orientalists in Europe. It has no support in any of sacred texts of the Hindus. "Hinduism" has been accepted *by usage* to stand for Sanātana Dharma particularly in its applications to the *viśeṣa dharma* of the Hindus.—Ed.

[1]In the whole of the RV there is not a single reference to any historical person or historical event, but all, as Sāyaṇa says, is eternal (*nityam*), the "past tense" present, past and future.

[2]"The charge of Pantheism that has been laid at his door is refuted by the very extravagance of the terms in which he asserts the Transcendence of the Godhead",— will apply equally to Eckhart and to Brahmanism. C.G. Roll, on Dionysius (1920, p. 34).

[3]*Karma* is the law of concordant action and reaction, and *Dharma* is inherent nature. One performs actions or acts in accordance with one's inherent nature.

Dharma is also *Lex aeterna*, ideal or absolute Justice or Righteousness, Greek *dikaiosynē* as in Plato and Luke 12.31; the proportionate part of this Justice, which pertains to an individual, is his 'own-justice' (*sva-dharma*), the vocation, social function, or duty as determined for him by his own nature.

See note 115 on Māyā in the section on 'Buddhism'.

return of deceased individuals to rebirth on this earth represents only a misunderstanding of the doctrines of heredity, transmigration and regeneration; and that the six *darśanas* of the later Sanskrit "philosophy" are not so many mutually exclusive "systems" but, as their name implies, so many "points of view" which are no more mutually contradictory than are, let us say, botany and mathematics. We shall also deny in Hinduism the existence of anything unique and peculiar to itself, apart from the local colouring and social adaptations that must be expected under the sun where nothing can be known except in the mode of the knower. The Indian tradition is one of the forms of the Philosophia Perennis, and as such, embodies those universal truths to which no one people or age can make exclusive claim. The Hindu is therefore perfectly willing to have his own scriptures made use of by others as "extrinsic and probable proofs" of the truth as *they* also know it. The Hindu would argue, moreover, that it is upon these heights alone that any true agreement of differing cultures can be effected.

We shall try now to state the fundamentals positively: not, however, as this is usually done in accordance with the "historical method"[4] by which the reality is more obscured than illuminated, but from a strictly orthodox point of view, both as to principles and their application; endeavouring to speak with mathematical precision, but never employing words of our own[5] or making any affirmation for which authority could not be cited by chapter and verse; in this way making even our technique characteristically Indian.

We cannot attempt a survey of the religious literature, since this would amount to a literary history of India, where we cannot say where what is sacred ends and what is secular begins, and even the songs of bayadères and showmen are the hymns of the Fidèles de l'Amour. Our literary sources begin with the Ṛgveda (1200 or more B.C.), and only end with the most modern Vaiṣṇava, Śaiva and Tantric theological treatises. We must, however, especially mention the *Bhagavad Gītā*[6] as probably the most important single work ever

[4]See René Guénon, *Introduction to the Study of the Hindu Doctrines*, London, 1945, p. 58. Cf. also *Walking on Water*, Willam N. Brown (Open Court, 1928), p. 17, note 24.

Where the date of a text need not be regarded as of importance for our purposes here. We have no intention to ignore the value of the "historical method" for some purposes; but do not think it is necessary in the exposition of doctrines, with which alone the present volume is concerned.

[5]"We shall fetch nothing from our own store"—Philo, *De Opificio Mundi*, I, 5.

"No pronouncement of a prophet is ever his own" —Philo, *De Specialibus Legibus*, IV, 49.

[6]". . . it may be said at once that amongst the sacred writings of mankind there is probably no other which is at once so great, so complete, and so short".—Sister Nivedita, *The Web of Indian Life*, ed. 1967 *Complete Works of Sister Nivedita*, Vol. II, p. 189.

produced in India; this book of eighteen chapters is not, as it has been sometimes called, a "sectarian" work, but one universally studied and often repeated daily from memory by millions of Indians of all persuasions; it may be described as a compendium of the whole Vedic doctrine to be found in the earlier Vedas, Brāhmaṇas and Upanishads, and being therefore the basis of all the later developments, it can be regarded as the focus of all Indian religion. To this we must add that the pseudo-historical Krishna and Arjuna are to be identified with the mythical Agni and Indra.

THE MYTH

Like the Revelation (*śruti*) itself, we must begin with the Myth (*itihāsa*), the penultimate truth, of which all experience is the temporal reflection. The mythical narrative is of timeless and placeless validity, true nowever[7] and everywhere: just as in Christianity, "In the beginning God created" and "Through him all things were made", regardless of the millenia that come between the datable words, amount to saying that the creation took place at Christ's "eternal birth". "In the beginning" (*agre*), or rather "at the summit", means "in the first cause": just as in our still told myths, "once upon a time" does not mean "once" alone, but "once for all".[8] The Myth is not a "poetic invention" in the sense these words now bear: on the other hand, and just because of its universality, it can be told, and with equal authority, from many different points of view.

In this everlasting beginning there is only the Supreme Identity of "That One" (*tad ekam*),[9] without differentiation of being from non-being, light from darkness, or separation of sky from earth. The All is for the present impounded in the first principle, which may be spoken of as the Person, Progenitor, Mountain, Tree, Dragon or endless Serpent. Related to this principle by filiation or younger brotherhood, and alter ego rather than another principle, is the Dragon-slayer, born to supplant the Father and take possession of the kingdom, distributing its treasures to his followers.[10] For if there is to be a world, the prison must be shattered and its potentialities liberated.

This can be done either in accordance with the Father's will or against his will; he may "choose death for his children's sake",[11] or it may be that the Gods impose the passion upon him, making him their sacrificial victim.[12] These are not contradictory doctrines, but different ways of telling one and the same story; in reality, Slayer and Dragon, sacrificer and victim are of one mind behind the scenes, where there is no incompatibility of contraries, but mortal enemies on the stage, where the everlasting war of the Gods[13] and the Titans

[7]With one "now" he has filled "always".—Plutarch, *Moralia* 393B.

[8]"At that time indeed, all things took shape simultaneously."—Philo, *De Op.* VII, 28, also Plotinus, *Enneads* VI.

[9]RV.X.129.1-3; TS.VI.4.8.3; JB.III.359; ŚB.X.5.3.1, 2, etc.

[10]RV.X.124.4, etc.

[11]RV.X.13.4, "They made Bṛhaspati the Sacrifice, Yama outpoured his own dear body."

[12]RV.X.90.6-8, "They made the first-born Person their sacrificial victim."

[13]The word *deva* like its cognates *theos, deus,* can be used in the singular to mean "God" or in the plural to mean "Gods" or sometimes "Angels"; just as we can say "Spirit" meaning the Holy Ghost, and also speak of spirits, and amongst others even of "evil spirits". The "Gods" of Proclus are the "Angels" of Dionysius. What may be called the "high Gods" are the Persons of the Trinity, Agni, Indra, Vāyu, Āditya, or Brahmā, Śiva,

is displayed. In any case, the Dragon-Father remains a Pleroma, no more diminished by what he exhales than he is increased by what he inhales. He is the Death, on whom our life depends;[14] and to the question "Is Death one, or many?" the answer is made that "He is one as he is there, but many as he is in his children here".[15] The Dragonslayer *is* already our Friend; the Dragon must be pacified and made a friend of.[16]

The passion is both an exhaustion and a dismemberment. The endless Serpent (*speirama aiōnos* coil of eternity), who for so long as he was one Abundance remained invincible,[17] is disjointed and dismembered as a tree is felled and cut up into logs.[18] For the Dragon, as we shall presently find, is also the World-Tree, and there is an allusion to the "wood" of which the world is made by the Carpenter.[19] The Fire of Life and Water of Life (Agni and Soma, the Dry and the Moist, ŚB.I.6.3.23), all Gods, all beings, sciences and goods are constricted by the Python, who as "Holdfast" (Namuci) will not let them go until he is smitten and made to gape and pant:[20] and from this Great Being, as if from a damp fire smoking, are exhaled the Scriptures, the Sacrifice, these worlds and all beings;[21] leaving him exhausted of his contents and like an empty skin.[22] In the same way the Progenitor, when he has emanated his children, is emptied out of all his possibilities of finite manifestation, and falls

---

Viṣṇu, to be distinguished only, and then not always sharply, from one another according to their functioning and spheres of operation. The *mixtae personae* of the dual Mitrāvarunau or Agnendrau are the form of the Sacerdotium and Regnum *in divinis*; their subjects, the "Many Gods", are the Maruts or Gales. The equivalents in ourselves are on the one hand the immanent median Breath, sometimes spoken of as Vamadeva, sometimes as Inner Man and Immortal Self, and on the other its extensions and subjects the Breaths, or powers of seeing, hearing, thinking, etc., of which our elemental "soul" is the unanimous composite, just as the body is a composite of functionally distinguishable parts that act in unison. The Maruts and the Breaths may act in obedience to their governing principle, or may rebel against it. All this is, of course, an over simplified statement. Cf. note 166 (Hinduism).

See Nicholson Studies . . . p. 153 Nafassu'l Rahman—"Universal breath of the Merciful".

[14]ŚB.X.5.2.13

[15]ŚB.X.5.2.16. Also *Enneades* IV.9.2; BG.XIII.27,30,16; XVIII.20.

[16]AB.III.4; TS.V.1.5,6; TS.VI.1.11.

[17]On "making a friend of " the Varuṇya agni or Soma who might otherwise destroy the Sacrificer, see AB.III.4; TS.V.1.5.6 and TS.VI.1.11.

[18]TA.V.1.3; MU.II.6(a).

[19]RV.I.32, etc.

[20]RV.X.31.7; X.81.4; TB.II.8.9,6; cf. RV.X.89.7; TS.VI.4.7.3.

[21]RV.I.54.5 *śvasanasya*. . . *śuṣṇasya*; RV.V.29.4 *svasantamava dānavam han*; TS.II.5.2.4 *jañjabhyamānad agniṣomau nirakrāmatām*; cf. ŚB.I.6.3.13-15; ŚB.V.5.5.1 "Of old everything here was within Vṛtra"; AB.III:20 *śvasasthāt* (*vṛtrasya*). JUB.I.47,3 All is Prajāpati's: *apāna*, expiration dying breath. BU.IV.5.11 *mahato bhūtasya* . . . *etāni sarvāṇi niḥśvasitāni*; M.U.VI.32, etc. "For all things arise out of only one being". (Also Behmen, *Sig. Rer.*XIV.74.) As in RV.X.90.

[22]ŚB.I.6.3.15,16.

down unstrung,[23] overcome by Death,[24] though he survives this woe.[25] Now the positions are reversed, for the Fiery Dragon will not and cannot be destroyed, but would enter into the Hero, to whose question "What, wouldst thou consume me?" it replies "Rather to kindle (waken, quicken) thee, that thou mayst eat".[26] The Progenitor, whose emanated children are as it were sleeping and inanimate stones, reflects "Let me enter into them, to awaken them";[27] but so long as he is one, he cannot, and therefore divides himself into the powers of perception and consumption, extending these powers from his hidden lair in the "cave" of the heart through the doors of the senses to their objects, thinking "Let me eat of these objects"; in this way "our" bodies are set up in possession of consciousness, he being their mover.[28] And since the Several Gods or Measures of Fire into which he is thus divided are "our" energies and powers, it is the same to say that "the Gods entered into man, they made the mortal their house".[29] His passible nature has now become

[23]"Is unstrung", *Vyasraṁsata,* i.e. is disjointed or dispersed so that having been jointless, he is articulated, having been one, is divided and overcome, like Makha (TA.V.1.3) and Vṛtra (originally jointless, RV.IV.19.3, but dissevered, I.32.7). For Prajāpati's fall and reconstitution see ŚB.I.6.3.35 and passim; PB.IV.10.1 and passim; TB.I.2.6.1; AA.III.2.6, etc. It is with reference to his "division" that in KU.V.4 the immanent deity (*dehin*) is spoken of as "unstrung" (*visraṁsamāna*); for he is one in himself, but many as he is in his children (ŚB.X.5.2.16) from out of whom he cannot easily come together again (see note 29).

[24]ŚB.X.4.4.1.

[25]PB.VI.5.1. (Prajāpati); cf. ŚB.IV.4.3.4 (Vṛtra). See also *Mahābhārata,* Vanaparva Ch. CLXXX.

[26]TS.II.4.12.6; ŚB.I.6.3.17. It is note worthy that whereas the "Person in the right eye" is usually spoken of as the Sun or solar Indra, it can equally well be said that it is Śuṣṇa (the Scorcher) that is smitten and when he falls enters into the eye as its pupil, or that Vṛtra becomes the right eye (ŚB.III.1.3.11,18). That is one of the many ways in which "Indra is now what Vṛtra was".

[27]ŚB.VIII.5.3.1 Indra and Prajāpati who enters into him with the essence of food.

[28]MU.II.6; cf. ŚB.III.9.1.2; JUB.I.46.1,2.

"Mover", as in Paradiso, I.116. *Questi nei cor mortali è permotore* (This is the motive force in mortal hearte). Cf. *Laws,* 898C. See Note 47.

[29]AV.XI.8.18; cf. ŚB.II.3.2.3; JUB.I.14.2, *mayy etās sarvā devatāḥ.* Cf. KB.VII.4 *ime puruṣe devatāḥ;* TS.VI.1.4.5 *prāṇā vai devā . . . teṣu parokṣaṁ juhoti* ("The Gods in this man . . . they are the Breaths . . . in them he sacrifices metaphysically"). See Patanjali's *Yoga Sutras* IV-23. "The mind, though assuming various forms by reason of innumerable mental deposits, exists for the purpose of the soul's emancipation and operates in cooperation therewith". Food is quite literally *consumed* by the digestive Fire: so, when a ritual meal is announced one should say "Kindle the Fire" (*samintsvāgnim,* JUB.II.15.1-3) or "Come to the feast" (*agne ā vītaye,* RV.VI.69.10, etc.) by way of benedicite.

KU.IV.6 (cf. Ait.Up.I.3.13).

Yaḥ pūrvam tapaso . . . ajāyata. guhām praviśya . . . bhutebhir vyapaśyata.

Colossians I.15 *primogenitus creaturae* (= the firstborn of every creature).

"ours": and from this predicament he cannot easily recollect or rebuild himself, whole and complete.[30]

We are now the stone from which the spark can be struck, the mountain beneath which God lies buried, the scaly reptilian skin that conceals him, and the fuel for his kindling. That his lair is now a cave or house presupposes the mountain or walls by which he is enclosed, *verborgen* and *verbaut*.[31] "You" and "I" are the psychophysical prison and Constrictor in whom the First has been swallowed up that "we" might be at all.[32] For as we are repeatedly told, the Dragon-slayer devours his victim, swallows him up and drinks him dry, and by this Eucharistic meal he takes possession of the first-born Dragon's treasure and powers and becomes what he was. We can cite, in fact, a remarkable text in which our composite is called the "mountain of God" and

---

Sig. Rer. III.38—"The Being of all beings, who thus manifests himself in particular beings with the eyes of eternity". Cf. Kaus.Up.II.13.

Climbing cf. JUB.I.33.1 (centre: summit: slope).

DhA.III.52—Mogallāna's plunge into earth and ascent Majjhena. Mt. Sineru.

[30]TS.V.5.2.1. *Prajāpatiḥ prajā sṛṣṭvā preṇānu praviśat, tābhyām punar sambhavitum nāśaknot;* Prajāpati after creating creatures in affection entered into them; from them he could not emerge again.

ŚB.I.6.3.36 *Sa visrastaiḥ parvabhiḥ na śaśāka samhātum* = He was unable to rise with his relaxed joints.

BU.IV.3.32 *salila eko dṛṣṭādvaito bhavati, eṣa brahmalokaḥ* KB.I.7.

Mil.263 *mahasannidohr*; 346 *dhamma-nadī* and *dhammasāgara*. *Mathnawī* III.4662—"Existence in non-existence is itself a marvel."

VI.1622—"opposites and likes in number as the leaves of the orchard, are as a fleck of foam on the Sea that hath no like or opposite".

VI.4052—"He that finds is lost: like a torrent he is absorbed in the Ocean."

V.802—"These footprints (extend) as far as the shore of the Ocean; then the footprints are naught in the Ocean."

II.160-1—"What is a Sufi's possession? Footprints."

[31]"Gott liegt verborgen und bedeckt im inwendigen Grunde".—Sermon 22 in W. Lehmann *Johannes Tauler Predigten,* Jena, 1917.

Sherman, *Philosophical Hymns*, p. 18 uses this word verborgen in the sense of Kath.Up.II.20 *nihito guhāyām* = is lodged in the heart.

[32]Philo, LA.III.74—"When the mind (nous) has carried off the prizes of virtue, it condemns the corpse body to death."

LA.I.108—"Now, when we are living, the soul is dead and has been entombed in the body as in a sepulchre; whereas, should we die, the soul lives forth with its own proper life, released from the body, the baneful corpse to which it was held."

Phaedrus, 250C—"entombed in the body".

Enneads, IV.8.3—"prison or tomb of the body, cavern or cave of Kosmos". The "cave" stands or mental activity as per the *Yoga Sutra* IV.23.

Cratylus, 400.C—"the body is the tomb of the soul".

RV.—*guhā niṣīdau* (*agni*).

Henry Constable—"Buryed in me, unto my sowle appeare." E Bk⁰ M⁰ veise p.13.

Eckhart, Pfeiffer, p. 593—"hat gewonet in uns verborgenliche". Trans. "has dwelt in us in a hidden manner".

we are told that the Comprehensor of this doctrine shall in like manner swallow up his own evil, hateful adversary.[33] This "adversary" is, of course, none but our self. The meaning of the text will only be fully grasped if we explain that the word for "mountain", *giri,* derives from the root *gir,* to "swallow".[34] Thus He in whom we were imprisoned is now our prisoner; as our Inner Man he is submerged in and hidden by our Outer Man. It is now his turn to become the Dragon-slayer; and in this war of the God with the Titan, now fought within you, where we are "at war with ourselves",[35] his victory and resurrection will be also ours, if we have known who we are. It is now for him to drink us dry, for us to be his wine.

We have realised that the deity is implicitly or explicitly a willing victim; and this is reflected in the human ritual, where the agreement of the victim, who must have been originally human, is always formally secured.[36] In either case

---

Kath. Up. III.12—"*Esa sarveṣu bhūteṣu gūḍho'tmā* . . .", "This Ātman, hidden in all beings . . .".

Philo, *Migr.* 188, 190—"man as troglodyte".

II *Cor.* 4.7—"But we have this treasure in earthen vessels, . . . "

Maitri Up. VI.28—"buried treasure".

[33]AA.II.1.8. St. Bonaventura likewise equated *mons* (noonlain) with *mens* (mind) (*De dec. praeceptis II, ascendere in montem, idest, in. eminentiam mentis*) (ascend the mountain which is the highest mind).

This traditional image which, like so many others, must be dated back to the time when "cave" and "home" were one and the same thing, underlies the familiar symbols of mining and seeking for buried treasure (CU.VIII.3.2; MU.VI.28, etc.). The powers of the soul (*bhūtāni,* a word that also means "gnomes") at work in the mind-mountain, are the types of the dwarf miners who protect the "Snow-White" Psyche when she has bitten into the fruit of good and evil and fallen into her death-like sleep, in which she remains until the divine Eros awakens her and the fruit falls from her lips. Whoever has understood the scriptural Mythos will recognize its paraphrases in the universal fairy-tales that were not created by, but have been inherited and faithfully transmitted by the "folk" to whom they were originally communicated. It is one of the prime errors of historical and rational analysis to suppose that the "truth" and "original form" of a legend can be separated from its miraculous elements. It is in the marvels themselves that the truth inheres:

"There is no other origin of philosophy than wonder", Plato, *Theatetus* 1556. And in the same way Aristotle who adds "therefore even a lover of fables is in a way a lover of wisdom, for fables are compounded of wonder" (*Metaphysics* 982B).

Myth embodies the nearest approach to absolute truth that can be stated in words.

[34]*Saṁyutta Nikāya,* III.86—"eaten up by my body, etc.".

There is a remarkable echo of the brahma-giri doctrine in *Majjhima Nikāya,* III.68 where the Isigiri pabbata in which the isī are living is so called in that it isī gilati, "swallows up the Rsis".

BU.III.2.13, *Śāṅkarabhāṣya—"grahātigraha lakśaṇena mṛtyunā grastam".*

[35]BG.VI.6; cf. S.I.57 = Dh.66; A.I.149; Rūmī, *Mathnawī* I.267f., etc.

[36]N.T. Romans, VII.24—"Who shall deliver me from the body of this death?" VI.6—". . . that the body of sin might be destroyed . . .". VIII.10—". . . the body is dead because of sin . . .".

the death of the victim is also its birth, in accordance with the infallible rule that every birth must have been preceded by a death: in the first case, the deity is multiply born in living beings, in the second they are reborn in him. But even so it is recognized that the sacrifice and dismemberment of the victim are acts of cruelty and even treachery;[37] and this is the original sin (*kilbiṣa*) of the Gods, in which all men participate by the very fact of their separate existence and their manner of knowing in terms of subject and object, good and evil, because of which the Outer Man is excluded from a direct participation in "what the Brāhmaṇas understand by Soma".[38] The form of our "knowledge", or rather "ignorance" (*avidyā*), dismembers him daily; and for this *ignorantia divisiva* an expiation is provided for in the Sacrifice, where by the sacrificer's surrender of himself and the building up again of the dismembered deity, whole and complete, the multiple selves are reduced to their single principle (consciously if they are "saved", unconsciously if they are "lost"). There is thus an incessant multiplication of the inexhaustible One and unification of the indefinitely Many. Such are the beginnings and endings of worlds and of individual beings: expanded from a point without position or dimensions and a now without date or duration, accomplishing their destiny, and when their time is up returning "home" to the Sea in which their life originated.[39]

[37]TS.II.5.1.2, II.5.3.6; cf.VI.4.8.1; ŚB.I.2.3.3, III.9.4.17; ŚB.XII.6.1.39,40; PB.XII.6.8,9; Kaus.Up.III.1, etc.; cf. Bloomfield in JAOS.XV.161.

[38]TS.II.4.12.1; AB.VII.28, etc.

[39]Mund.Up.III.2.8; Praśna Up.VI.5; A.IV.198, Udāna 55. For further parallels see *Review of Religion*, Nov. 1941, p.18, note 2.

For the return of the "Rivers" to the "Sea" in which their individuality is merged, so that one speaks only of the "Sea": CU.VI.10.1, Praśna Up.VI.5, Mund. Up.III.2.8, A.IV.198, Udāna 55, and similarly Lao Tzu, *Tao Te Ching* XXXII, Rūmī, *Mathnawī* VI.4052, Meister Eckhart (in Pfeiffer's edn., p. 314), . . . all to the effect that "As the drop becomes the ocean, so the soul is deified, losing her name and work, but not her essence" (Angelus Silesius, *Cherubinische Wandersmann* II.15): "And in his will is our tranquility:/It is the mighty ocean, whither tends/Whatever it creates and nature makes" (Dante, *Paradiso* III.85.86).

For "going home" (to Agni) RV.I.66.5; V.2.6; (to Brahmā) MU.VI.22; (to the "Sea") Praśna Up.VI.5; (to the Gale) RV.X.16.3; AV.X.8.16 (like Katha Up.IV.9; BU.I.5.23), JUB.III.1.1,2,3,12; CU.IV.3.1-3; (to the *summum bonum*, man's last end) S.IV.158; Sn.1074-6; Mil.73); (to our Father) Luke 23.46.

Eckhart I.176—"the sea of his own unfathomable nature". *Mathnawī* IV.2062—"Silence is the Sea and speech is like the river"; Rumi Odes, XII, XV; BU.IV.3.32; Kaus.Up.I.7. *Majjhima Nikāya* I.488—Buddha like *mahāsamudda,* fathomless, etc. I.494—Like river to sea every pilgrim tends towards *nibbāna.*

Saṁyutta Nikāya IV.179-80—gliding downstream to *nibbāna.*

THEOLOGY AND AUTOLOGY[40]

The Sacrifice (*yajña*) undertaken here below is a ritual mimesis of what was done by the Gods in the beginning, and in the same way both a sin and an expiation. We shall not understand the Myth until we have made the Sacrifice, nor the Sacrifice until we have understood the Myth. But before we can try to understand the operation it must be asked, what is God? and what are we?

God is an essence without duality (*advaita*), or as some maintain, without duality but not without relations (*visiṣṭādvaita*). He is only to be apprehended as Essence (*asti*),[41] but this Essence subsists in a two-fold nature (*dvaitibhāva*);[42] as being and as becoming.[43] Thus, what is called the Entirety (*kṛtsnam, pūrṇam, bhūman*) is both explicit and inexplicit (*niruktānirukta*), sonant and silent (*śabdāśabda*), characterized and uncharacterized (*saguṇa, nirguṇa*), temporal and eternal (*kālākāla*), partite and impartite (*sakalākāla*), in a likeness and not in any likeness (*mūrtāmūrta*), shewn and unshewn (*vyaktāvyakta*), mortal and immortal (*martyāmartya*), perishable and the Imperishable (*kṣaraścākṣarn*), and so forth. Whoever knows him in his proximate (*apara*) aspect, immanent, knows him also in his ultimate (*para*) aspect, transcendent;[44] the Person seated in our heart, eating and drinking, is also the Person in the Sun.[45] This Sun of men, and Light of lights[46] "whom all men see but few know with the mind",[47] is the Universal Self (*ātman*) of all things mobile or immobile.[48] He is both inside and outside (*bahir antaś ca*

[40]Autology (Chambers, 1983-edn.) has been defined as "knowledge or understanding of oneself" (*heautou epistēmē, ātmavidyā, ātmajñāna*), not like other sciences, but the science of itself and of other sciences. See Plato—*Charmides* 165D, 166E; *Republic* 430, 432 and *Sophroniscus* in Plato's notes.

[41]KU.VI.13; MU.IV.4, etc.

[42]ŚB.X.1.4.1; BU.II.3; MU.VI.15, VII.11. No trace of Monophysitism or of Patripassianism can be discovered in the so-called "monism" of the Vedanta; the "non-duality" being that of two natures coincident without composition.

[43]Being and becoming, *tattva* and *bhava* correspond to Gk. *ousia* (= being) and *nemesis* (= personification of divine wrath).

[44]MU.VI.22; Praś.Up.V.2.

[45]BU.IV.4.24; Tait.Up.III.10.4; MU.VI.1.2.

[46]RV.I.113.1, I.146.4; BU.IV.1.6; Mund.Up.II.2.9; BG.XIII.17; John I.4.

[47]AV.X.8.14; Plato, *Laws* 898 D. "Since soul is what, so it seems to us, makes everything go round."

Every one sees the body of the sun, but no one sees his soul,—See Jewett's translation of the Dialogues of Plato, Vol. I, p. 640.

[48]RV.I.115.1, VII.101.6; AV.X.8.44; AA.III.2.4.

Autology (*ātma-jñāna*) is the fundamental theme of scripture; but it must be understood that this Self-knowledge differs from any empirical knowledge of an object in as much as our Self is always the subject and can never become the object of

bhutānām), but uninterruptedly (*anantaram*), and therefore a total presence, undivided in divided things.[49] He does not come from anywhere,[50] nor does he become anyone,[51] but only lends himself to all possible modalities of existence.[52]

The question of his names, such as Agni, Indra, Prajāpati, Śiva, Brahmā, etc.,[53] whether personal or essential, is dealt with in the usual way: "they call

---

knowledge; in other words, all definition of the ultimate Self must be by remotion.

Ātman (root *an,* to breathe, cf. *atmos, autmē* is primarily Spiritus, the luminous and pneumatic principle, and as such often equated with the Gale (*Vāyu, Vāta,* root *vā,* to blow) of the Spirit which "bloweth as it listeth" (*yathā vaśam carati,* RV.X.168.4 as in John III.8). Being the ultimate in all things, *ātman* acquires the secondary sense of "Self", regardless of our level of reference, which may be either somatic, psychic or spiritual. So that over against our real Self, the Spirit in ourselves and all living things there is the "self", of which we speak when we say "I" or "you", meaning this or that man, so-and-so. In other words there are two in us, Outer and Inner Man, psycho-physical personality and very Person. It is therefore according to the context that we must translate. Because the word *ātman,* used reflexively, can only be rendered by "self" we have adhered to the sense of "self" throughout, distinguishing Self from self by the capital, as is commonly done. But it must be clearly understood that the distinction is really of "spirit" (pneuma) from "soul" (psyche) in the Pauline sense. It is true that the ultimate Self, "this self's immortal Self" (MU.III.2, VI.2), is identical with Philo's "soul of the soul" (psyche, psyches), and with Plato's "immortal soul" as distinguished from the "mortal soul" and that some translators render *ātman* by "soul"; but although there are contexts in which "soul" means "spirit" (cf. William of Thierry, *Epistle to the Brethren of Mont Dieu,* Ch. XV, on this very problem of the distinction of *anima* from *animus*; see also Philo, *Heres* 55) it becomes dangerously misleading, in view of our current notions of "psychology" to speak of the ultimate and universal Self as a "soul". It would be, for example, a very great mistake to suppose that when a "philosopher" such as Jung speaks of "man in search of a soul" this has anything whatever to do with the Indian search for the Self, or for that matter with the injunction, *Gnōthi seauton,* know thy Self. The empiricist's "self" is for the metaphysician, just like all the rest of our environment, "not my Self".

Of the two "selves" referred to, the first is born of woman, the second of the divine womb, the sacrificial fire (ŚB.I.8.3.6; and whoever has not thus been "born again" is effectively possessed of but the one and mortal self that is born of the flesh and must end with it (JB.I.17, cf. John III.6, Gal.VI.8, I Cor.15.50, etc.). Hence in the Upanishads and Buddhism the fundamental questions "Who art thou?", and "By which self?" is immortality attainable, the answer being, only by that Self that *is* immortal; the Indian texts never fall into the error of supposing that a soul that has had a beginning in time can also be immortal; nor indeed, can we see that the Christian Gospels anywhere put forward such an impossible doctrine as this.

[49]BG.XIII.15,16; XV.16,17; XVIII.20. *uttamaḥ puruṣastvanyaḥ.*

[50]Cf. John III.18.

[51]KU.II.18.

[52]BU.IV.4.5.

[53]See AB.IV.22 on Names. The following correspondences of names and functions have been drawn—Agni: sacerdotium, Indra: regnum, Prajāpati: progenitor, Śiva: king, Brahmā: lordship.

him many who is really one";[54] "even as he seems, so he becomes";[55] "he takes the forms imagined by his worshippers".[56] The trinitarian names—Agni, Vāyu and Āditya or Brahmā, Rudra and Vishnu—"are the highest embodiments of the supreme, immortal, bodiless Brahma—their becoming is a birth from one another, partitions of a common Self defined by its different operations—These embodiments are to be contemplated, celebrated, and at last recanted. For by means of them one rises higher and higher in the worlds; but where the whole ends, attains the simplicity of the Person."[57] Of all the names and forms of God the monogrammatic syllable Aum, the totality of all sounds and the music of the spheres chanted by the resonant Sun, is the best. The validity of such an audible symbol is exactly the same as that of a plastic icon, both alike serving as supports of contemplation (*dhiyālamba*); such a support is needed because that which is imperceptible to eye or ear cannot be apprehended objectively as it is in itself, but only in a likeness. The symbol must be naturally adequate, and cannot be chosen at random; one locates or infers (*āveṣyati, āvāhayati*) the unseen in the seen, the unheard in the heard; but these forms are only means by which to approach the formless and must be discarded before we can become it.

Whether we call him Person, or Sacerdotium, or Magna Mater, or by any other grammatically masculine, feminine or neuter names, "That" (*tat, tadekam*) of which our powers are measures (*tanmātrā*) is a syzygy of conjoint principles, without composition or duality.[58] These conjoint principles or selves, indistinguishable ab intra, but respectively self-sufficient and insufficient ab extra, become contraries only when we envisage the act of self-manifestation (*svaprakāśatvam*) implied when we descend from the silent level of the Non-duality to speak in terms of subject and object and to recognize the many separate and individual existences that the All (*Sarvam* = *to pan*) or Universe (*viśvam*) presents to our physical organs of perception. And since this finite totality can be only logically and not really divided from its infinite source, "That One" can also be called an "Integral Multiplicity"[59] and "Omniform Light".[60] Creation is exemplary. The conjoint principles, for example, Heaven and Earth, or Sun and Moon, man and woman, were originally one. Ontologically, their conjugation (*mithunam, sambhava, eko bhava*) is a vital operation, productive of a third in the image of the first and nature of the second. Just as the conjugation of Mind (*manas*) with the Voice (*vāc*) gives birth to a concept (*saṅkalpa*) so the conjugation of Heaven and Earth kindles the Bambino, the Fire, whose birth divides his parents from one another and

[54]RV.X.114.5, cf. III.5.4, V.3.1.

[55]RV.V.44.6.

[56]*Kailayamālai* (see *Ceylon National Review*, no. 3, 1907, p. 280).

[57]*Nirukta* VII.4; *Bṛhad Devatā* I.70-4; MU.IV.6.

[58]"There is no distinction of elder or younger between One and another."—*Liturgical Homilies of Narsai.* (Trans. Dom Connolly, Camb. Univ. Press, 1909.), Homily XXII.

[59]RV.III.54.8 *viśvam ekam.*

[60]VS.V.35 *jyotir asi viśvarūpam.*

fills the intervening Space (*antarikṣa*, Midgard) with light;[61] and in the same way microcosmically, being kindled in the space of the heart, he is its light. He shines in his Mother's womb,[62] in full possession of all his powers.[63] He is no sooner born than he traverses the Seven Worlds,[64] ascends to pass through the Sun-door, as the smoke from an altar or central hearth, whether without or within you, ascends to pass out through the eye of the dome.[65] This Agni is at once the messenger of God, the guest in all men's houses, whether constructed or bodily, the luminous pneumatic principle of life, and the missal priest who conveys the savour of the Burnt-offering hence to the world beyond the vault of the Sky, through which there is no other way but this "Way of the Gods" (*devayāna*). This Way must be followed by the Forerunner's footprints, as the word for "Way"[66] itself reminds us, by all who would reach the "farther shore" of the luminous spatial river of life[67] that divides this terrestrial from yonder celestial strand; these conceptions of the Way underlying all the detailed symbolisms of the Voyage and the Pilgrimage, Bridge and Active Door.

Considered apart, the "halves" of the originally undivided Unity can be distinguished in various ways according to our point of view; politically, for example, as Sacerdotium and Regnum (*brahma-kṣatrau*), and psychologically as Self and Not-self, Inner Man and Outer Individuality, Male and Female. These pairs are disparate; and even when the subordinate has been separated from the superior with a view to productive cooperation, it still remains in

[61]For *vāc as logos* and the creation of the triple science, see ŚB.VI.1.1.9-10.

manas = *nous* -mind, *logos* -word, *dianoia* -thought; *vāc* = *hermēneia* -interpretation, *psuche* -soul, *aisthēsis* -sense perception; *saṅkalpa*= *alētheia* -truth, *doxe* -opinion, *sophia* -wisdom.

On *nous* (mind) and *ēcho* (sound) see Philo, *De migr.* 83

On *aisthēsis* and *psuche, doxe* see Philo LA.III.221.

[62]RV.VI.16.35, cf. III.29.14.

[63]RV.III.3.10, RV.X.115.1, etc.

[64]RV.X.8.4, RV.X.122.3.

[65]For the Sun-door, the "ascent after Agni" (TS.V.6.8; AB.IV.20-2), etc., see my "Svayamatṛṇṇā; Janua Coeli" in *Zalmoxis* II, 1939 (1941).

[66]*Mārga*, "Way", from *mṛg* = *ichneuō*, to track, hunt. The doctrine of the vestigia pedis is common to Greek, Christian, Hindu and Buddhist teaching and is the basis of the iconography of the "footprints". The forerunners can be traced by their spoor as far as the Sundoor, Janua Coeli, the End of the Road; beyond that they cannot be tracked.

Phaedrus 266B—"I follow this one in his tracks as if he were a god;" and *Phaedrus* 253A—"tracking on their own accord"; also *Mathnawī* II.160.1—"What is the Sufi's provision? Footprints. He stalks the game like a hunter: he sees the musk deer's track and follows the footprints". Cf. *The Original Gospel of Buddhism* (Rhys Davids), No. 680, and MU; *Matallao,* to search after other things, to explore carefully. Cf. also Psalm 123.6 "My soul has been delivered as a sparrow out of the snare of the fowlers." The symbolism of tracking like that of "error" (sin) as a "failure to hit the mark", is one of those that have come down to us from the oldest hunting cultures. See note 13.

[67]*Lo gran mar d'essere*, 'through the vast sea of being', *Paradiso* I.113. The "crossing" is the *diaposeia of Plato's Epinomis* 986E.

the latter, more eminently. The Sacerdotium, for example, is "both the Sacerdotium and the Regnum"—a condition found in the *mixta persona* of the priest-king Mitrāvaruṇau, or Indrāgnī—but the Regnum as a separated function is nothing but itself, relatively feminine, and subordinated to the Sacerdotium, its Director (*netṛ = hegemon*). Mitra and Varuṇa correspond to *para* and *apara* Brahmā, and just as Varuṇa is feminine to Mitra, so the functional distinction in terms of sex defines the hierarchy. God himself is male to all, but just as Mitra is male to Varuṇa and Varuṇa in turn male to Earth, so the Priest is male to the King, and the King male to his realm. In the same way the man is subject to the joint government of Church and State; but in authority with respect to his wife, who in turn administers his estate. Throughout the series it is the noetic principle that sanctions or enjoins what the aesthetic performs or avoids; disorder arising only when the latter is distracted from her rational allegiance by her own ruling passions and identifies this subjection with "liberty".[68]

The most pertinent application of all this is to the individual, whether man or woman: the outer and active individuality of "this man or woman, so-and-so" being naturally feminine and subject to its own inner and contemplative Self. On the one hand, the submission of the Outer to the Inner Man is all that is meant by the words "self-control" and "autonomy", and the opposite of what is meant by "self-assertion": and on the other, this is the basis of the interpretation of the return to God in terms of an erotic symbolism, "As one embraced by a darling bride knows naught of 'I' and 'thou', so the self embraced by the foreknowing (solar) Self knows naught of a 'myself' within or a 'thyself' without;"[69] because, as Śankara remarks, of "unity". It is this Self that the man who really loves himself or others, loves in himself and in them; "all things are dear only for the sake of Self".[70] In this true love of Self the distinction of "selfishness" from "altruism" loses all its meaning. He sees the Self, the Lord, alike in all beings, and all beings alike in that Lordly Self.[71] "Loving thy Self", in the words of Meister Eckhart, "thou lovest all men as thy Self".[72] All these doctrines coincide with the Sūfī, "What is Love? Thou shalt know when thou becomest me".[73]

[68]For this whole paragraph see my "*Spiritual Authority and Temporal Power in the Indian Theory of Government*", American Oriental Society, 1942 (2nd edn. IGNCA).

[69]BU.IV.3.21 (rather freely translated), cf. BU.I.4.3; CU.VII.25.2. See *Meister Eckhart*, trans. by Evans, I, p. 368—"In the embrace of this sovran One that naughts the separated self of things, being is one without distinction . . .". We are repeatedly told that the deity is "both within and without", i.e. immanent and transcendent; in the last analysis this theological distinction breaks down, and "Whoever is joined unto the Lord is *one* spirit" (I Cor. 6.17).

[70]BU.II.4, etc. On true "Self-Love" see references in HJAS.4, 1939, p.135 and note.

[71]BG.VI.29, XIII.27.

[72]Meister Eckhart, Evans trans., Vol. I, p. 239; cf. *Sutta Nipata* 705 and also Von Hilderbrand (Longman Green, 1943), *Lilurgy and Personality*, p. 55.

[73]*Mathnawī*, Bk.II. Introduction. See also note 202 (Hinduism).
Sum. Theol. II-II.25.7 "union of wills".

The sacred marriage, consummated in the heart, adumbrates the deepest of all mysteries.[74] For this means both our death and beatific resurrection. The word to "marry" (*eko bhū*, become one) also means to "die", just as in Greek, *teleo* is to be perfected, to be married, or to die. When "Each is both", no relation persists: and were it not for this beatitude (*ānanda*) there would be neither life nor gladness anywhere.[75] All this implies that what we call the world-process and a creation is nothing but a game (*krīḍā, līlā, paidia, dolce gioco*) that the Spirit plays with itself, and as sunlight "plays" upon whatever it illuminates and quickens, although unaffected by its apparent contacts. We who play the game of life so desperately for temporal stakes might be playing at love with God for higher stakes—ourselves, and his. We play against one another for possessions, who might be playing with the King who stakes his throne and what is his against our lives and all we are: a game in which the more is lost, the more is won.[76]

By the separation of Heaven and Earth the "Three Worlds" are distinguished; the in-between World (*antarikṣa*) provides the etherial space (*ākāśa*)[77] in which the inhibited possibilities of finite manifestation can take birth in accordance with their several natures. From this first etherial

---

Shams-i-Tabriz Ode XIII, "What is Love".
Behmen, passim "God, the Being of all beings".
Jacofrom da Todi—"He and the soul are interfused . . .".

"But if I live, and yet not I,
Have being, yet not mine,
This one-in-twain and twain-in-one
How shall my words define?"

[74]ŚB.X.5.2.11-12; BU.IV.3.21, etc.

[75]TU.II.7,8.

[76]For this whole paragraph see my "Lila" in JAOS.61, 1940. (Also in Selected Papers, Vol. II.)

"Thou didst contrive this 'I' and 'we' in order that
thou mightest play the game of worship with Thyself,
That all 'I's' and 'thou's' should become one life."

Rūmī, *Mathnawī* I.1787.

Per sua diffalta in pianta ed in affamo
Cambio onesto riso e dolce gioco,
"through his fault he had a short stay here
through his fault he exchanged honesty joy and sweet sport for tears and toil.

Dante, *Purgatorio* XXVIII.95,96.

Also Plotinus, *Enneads.* IV.7.2 and Philo, *Heres* 282-3.

Near as they can, approaching; and they can
The more, the loftier their vision. Those
That round them fleet, gazing the Godhead next,

[77]Mund.Up.II.1.3, ŚB.I.4.1.23 *agne ā vītaye*, etc. RV.VIII.16.6 *varivaskṛt.*

substance are derived in succession air, fire, water and earth; and from these five elemental Beings (*bhūtāṇi*), combined in various proportions, are formed the inanimate bodies of creatures;[78] into which the God enters to awaken them, dividing himself to fill these worlds and to become the "Several Gods", his children.[79] These Intelligences[80] are the host of "Beings" (*bhūtagaṇa*) that operate in us, unanimously, as our "elemental soul" (*bhuūtātman*), or conscious self;[81] our "selves", indeed, but for the present mortal and unspiritual (*anātmya, anātman*), ignorant of their immortal Self (*ātmānam ananuvidya, anātmajña*),[82] and to be distinguished from the Immortal deities who have already become what they are by their "worth" (*arhaṇa*) and are spoken of as "Arhats" (= "Dignities").[83] Through the mundane and perfectible deities, and just as a King receives tribute (*balim āhṛ*) from his subjects,[84] the Person in the heart, our Inner Man who is also the Person in the Sun (MU.VI.1,2), obtains the food (*anna, āhāra*), both physical and mental, on which he must subsist when he proceeds from being to becoming. And because of the simultaneity of his dynamic presence in all past and future becomings,[85] the emanated powers at work in our consciousness can be regarded as the temporal support of the solar Spirit's timeless providence (*prajñāna*) and omniscience (*sarvajñāna*). Not that this sensible world of successive events determined by mediate causes (*karma, adṛṣṭa, apūrva*) is the source of his knowledge, but rather that it is itself the consequence of the Spirit's awareness of "the diversified world picture painted by itself on the vast canvas of itself."[86] It is not

[78]CU.I.9.1, VIII.14, VII.12.1, V.15.2; TU.II.1.1; ŚB.XI.2.3.4-5. Space, Ether is the origin and end of "name and aspect", i.e. of existence; the four other elements arise from it and return to it as to their prior. When, as often in Buddhism, account is taken only of four elements, these are the concrete bases of material things. Cf. St. Bonaventura, *On the Reduction of Art to Theology*, 3, Quinque sunt corpora mundi simplicia, scilcet quatuor elementa et quinta essentia (the body of the world can be reduced to five things, four elements and the fifth, essence).

Just as also in early Greek philosophy the "four roots" or "elements" (fire, air, earth and water of Empedokles, and *Timaeus* 32, 33-52 where at the divine Nature, Māyā, is described as chora, void of all forms) do not include the spatial ether, while Plato mentions all five (*Epinomis* 981C), and as Hermes points out "the existence of all things that are would have been impossible, if space had not existed as an antecedent condition of their being" (Ascl.II.15). It would be absurd to suppose that those who speak only of four "elements" were not conscious of this rather obvious consideration.

[79]MU.II.6, VI.26; that is to say, apparently (iva) divided in things divided, but really undivided (BG.XIII.16, XVIII.20), cf. Hermes *Lib.* X.7 where "souls are 'so to speak'" (*hōsper* = as if) parcelled out and partitioned off from the one All Soul.

[80]*Jñānāni, prajñā-mātrā*, etc., KU.VI.10; MU.VI.30; Kaus. Up.III.8.

[81]MU.III.2f.

[82]ŚB.II.2.2.8; XI.2.3.6, etc. Cf. notes 50 and 56 in section on Buddhism.

[83]RV.V.86.5, X.63-4, etc.

[84]AV.X.7.39, XI.4.19; JUB.IV.23.7; BU.IV.3.37, 38, etc.

[85]RV.X.90.2; AV.X.8.1; KU.IV.13; Svet.Up.III.15, etc.

[86]Śaṅkarāchārya, *Svātmanirūpana*, 95. The "world-picture" (*Sūryaśataka* 26—

by means of this All that he knows himself, but by his knowledge of himself that he becomes this All.[87] To know him by this All belongs only to *our* inferential manner of knowing.[88]

You must have begun to realise that the theology and the autology are one and the same science, and that the only possible answer to the question, "What am I?" must be "That art thou".[89] For as there are two in him who is both Love and Death,[90] so there are, as all tradition affirms unanimously, two in us; although not two of him or two of us, nor even one of him and one of us, but only one of both. As we stand now, in between the first beginning and the last end, we are divided against ourselves, essence from nature, and therefore see him likewise as divided against himself and from us. Let us describe the situation in two different figures. Of the conjugate birds, Sunbird and Soulbird, that perch on the Tree of Life, one is all-seeing, the other eats of its fruits.[91] For the Comprehensor these two birds are one;[92] in the iconography we find either one bird with two heads, or two with necks entwined. But from our point of view there is a great difference between the spectator's and the participant's lives; the one is not involved, the other, submerged in her

---

jagaccitra = *chosmos noētos*, intelligible world order) may be called the form of the divine omniscience, and is the paradigm, apart from time, of all existence, the "creation" being exemplary. See my "Vedic Exemplarism" in HJAS.I,1936. "A precursor of the Indo-Iranian *arta* and even of the Platonic idea is found in the Sumerian *gish-ghar*, the outline, plan, or pattern of things-which-are-to-be, designed by the Gods at the creation of the world and fixed in the heaven in order to determine the immutability of their creation" (Albright in JAOS.54, 1934, p. 130, cf. p. 121, note 48). The "world picture" is Plato's *paradeigma aiōna*, eternal paradigm (*Timaeus* 29A, 37C), Hermes' *to archetupon eidas* the archetypal form (*Lib.*I.8) and St. Augustine's "eternal mirror which leads the minds of those who look in it to a knowledge of all creatures, and better than elsewhere". See Bissen, *L'Exemplarisme divin selon St. Bonaventura*, 1929, p. 39, note 5); cf. St. Thomas Aquinas, *Sum. Theol.* I.12.9 and 10, "But all things are seen in God as in a certain intelligible mirror, not successively, but simultaneously." "When the body-dweller, controlling the powers of the soul that seize upon what is their own in sounds, etc., glows, then he sees the Spirit (*ātman*) extended in the world in the Spirit" (*Mahābhārata* III.210); "I behold the world as a picture, the Spirit" (*Siddhāntamuktāvalī*, p.181).

[87]BU.I.4.10, Praś.IV.10. Omniscience presupposes omnipresence, and conversely.

[88]Bonaventura: *On the Reduction of Art to Theology*—10, "Behold, how divine wisdom is secretly contained in sensitive knowledge." Dante, *Paradiso*, I.116—"This moves the hearts of mortal animals." St. Thomas Aquinas, *Sum. Theol.* I-II.68.4 ad 31—"The Holy Spirit is the principal mover. . . . Men, who are in a manner His instrument, as they are moved by Him."

[89]SA.XIII; CU.VI.8.7, etc.

[90]TS.III.4.7, Mṛtyu and Kāma amongst the components of the Gandharva, the Presiding Deity of the sacrifice.

[91]RV.I.164.20; Mund.Up.III.1.1-3.

[92]RV.X.114.5.

feeding and nesting, grieves for her lack of lordship (*anīśa*) until she perceives her Lord (*īśa*), and recognizes her Self in him and in his majesty, whose wings have never been clipped.[93]

In another way, the constitution of worlds and of individuals is compared to a wheel (*cakra*), of which the hub is the heart, the spokes powers, and their points of contact on the felly, our organs of perception and action.[94] Here the "poles" that represent our selves, respectively profound and superficial, are the motionless axle-point on which the wheel revolves—"Due from the pole, round which the first wheel rolls"[95]—and the rim in contact with the earth to which it reacts. This is the "wheel of becoming, or birth" (*bhava cakra* = *ho trochos tes geneseōs* = the round of generation)[96]. The collective motion of all the wheels within wheels—each one turning on a point without position and one and the same in all—that are these worlds and individuals is called the Confluence (*samsāra*), and it is in this "storm of the world's flow" that our "elemental self" (*bhūtātman*) is fatally involved: fatally, because whatever "we" are naturally "destined" to experience under the sun is the ineluctable consequence of the uninterrupted but unseen operation of mediate causes (karma, adṛṣṭa), from which only the aforesaid "point" remains independent, being in the wheel indeed, but not a "part" of it.

It is not only *our* passible nature that is involved, but also *his*. In this compatible nature he sympathizes with our miseries and our delights and is subjected to the consequences of things done as much as "we" are. He does not choose his wombs, but enters into births that may be aughty or naughty (*sadasat*)[97] and in which his mortal nature is the fructuary (*bhoktṛ*) equally of good and evil, truth and falsity.[98] That "he is the only seer, hearer, thinker, knower and fructuary" in us,[99] and that "whoever sees, it is by his ray that he sees",[100] who (*Īkṣvaku*) looks forth in all beings, is the same as to say that "the Lord is the only transmigrator",[101] and it follows inevitably that by the very act

[93]Mund.Up.III.1.1-3.

[94]BU.II.5.15, IV.4.22; Kaus.Up.III.8, etc.; similarly Plotinus, *Enneads*, VI.5.5.

[95]*Paradiso*, XIII.11,12—"*il punto dello stelo al cui la prima rota va dintorno*".

[96]James 3.6. See also Sermon on Fire in Vinaya Piṭaka; Philo, Somn.II.44—*kuklon kai trochon anangkēs ateleutētou* = a circlet and hoop of endless necessity; distinguished from the chain of Nature's activities; and *heirmon ton tes phuseos, pragmaton* = *hormiskos* given to Tamas.

And Boehme *De incarnatione Verbi* II.10.4 "Wheel of Nature".

[97]MU.III.2; BG.XIII.21.

[98]MU.II.6, VII.11.8. See my "*Spiritual Authority and Temporal Power*...", 1942-edn., p. 74 —the distinction of *satya* from *anṛta*.

[99]AA.III.2.4; BU.III.8.11, IV.5.15, etc.

[100]JUB.I.28.8, and similarly for the other powers of the soul.

[101]Śāṅkarācārya on *Brahmā Sutra* I.1.5, *satyam neśvarād anyaḥ saṁsāri*: this very important affirmation is amply supported by earlier texts, e.g. RV.VIII.43.9, X.72.9; AV.X.8.13; BU.III.7.23, III.8.11, IV.3.37,38; Svet.Up.II.16, IV.11; MU.V.2, etc. See also my, "On the One and Only Transmigrant" in JAOS, Supplement No. 3, Apr.-June 1944. There is no individual transmigrant essence. Cf. John III.13 "No man hath

with which he endows us with consciousness "he fetters himself like a bird in the net", and is subject to the evil, Death,[102]—or *seems* to be thus fettered and subjected.

Thus he is apparently submitted to our ignorance and suffers for our sins. Who then can be liberated and by whom and from what? It would be better to ask, with respect to this absolutely unconditional liberty, What is free now and nowever from the limitations that are presupposed by the very notion of individuality (*aham ca mama ca*, "I and mine"; *karta'ham iti*, "'I' am a doer")?[103] Freedom is from one's self, this "I", and its affections. He only *is* free from

ascended up to heaven, but he that came down from heaven, even the Son of (the) Man which is in heaven." The figure of the land-leech in BU.IV.4.3 does not imply the passing over from one body to another of an individual life other than that of the universal Spirit but only of a "part as it were" of this Spirit wrapped up in the activities that occasion the prolongation of becoming (Śaṅkarācārya, *Brahmā Sutra* II.3.43, III.1.1). In other words, life is renewed by the living Spirit of which the seed is the vehicle, while the nature of this life is determined by the properties of the seed itself (BU.III.9.28, Kaus.Up.III.3 and similarly St. Thomas Aquinas, *Sum. Theol.* III.32.11) and so as Blake expresses it, "Man is born like a garden, ready planted and sown." All that we inherit from our ancestors is a character; the Sun is our real Father. Accordingly, as in JUB.III.14.10, M.I.265/6, and Aristotle, *Physica* II.2—*anthropos gar anthropon genna helios* (- Man is begotten by man and by the sun as well) as rightly understood by St. Thomas Aquinas, *Sum. Theol.* I.115.3 ad 2, and Dante, De monarchia IX, cf. St. Bonaventura, *On the Reduction of Art to Theology*, 20 [Wicksteed's and Cornford's remarks in the Loeb Library Physics, p.126, shows that they have not grasped the doctrine itself].

[102]ŚB.X.4.4.1.

[103]BG.III.27, XVIII.17; cf. JUB.I.5.2; BU.III.7.23; MU.VI.30, etc. Similarly S.II.252; Udāna 70, etc. To the conceit " 'I' am" (*asmi-māna*) and " 'I' do" (*kartā'ham iti*) corresponds Greek *oiēsis* = *doxa* (Phaedrus 92A, 244C). For Philo, this *oiēsis* is "akin to untaught ignorance" (I.93); the mind that says "I plant" is impious (I.53); "I deem nothing so shameful as to suppose that *I* exert my mind or my sense" (I.78). Plutarch couples *oiēma* with *tuphos* (II.39D). It is from the same point of view that St. Thomas Aquinas says that "In so far as men are sinners they do not exist at all" (*Sum. Theol.* I.20.2 ad 4); and in accordance with the axiom Ens et bonum convertuntur (= the being of a thing is itself a good),—that *sat* and *asat* are not only "being" and "non-being" but also "good" and "evil" (e.g. in MU.III.1 and BG.XIII.21). Whatever "we" do more or less than correctly is "amiss" and should only be regarded as a thing not done at all. For example "What in the laud falls short is not-lauded, what is over-much is ill-lauded, what is exactly lauded is actually lauded" (JB.I.356). That what is not done "right" might as well not have been done at all, and is strictly speaking "not an act" (*akṛtam*, "unthat"), underlies the tremendous emphasis that is laid upon the notion of a "correct" performance of rites or other actions. The final result is that "we" are the authors of whatever is done amiss, and therefore not really "done" at all; while of whatever is actually done, God is the author. Just as in our own experience, if I make a table that does not stand, I am "no carpenter", and the table not really a table; while if I make a real table, it is not by my self as this man but "by art" that the table is really made, "I" being only an efficient cause. In the same way the Inner Person is distinguished from the elemental self as promoter (*kārayitṛ*) from operator (*kartṛ*,

virtues and vices and all their fatal consequences who never became anyone; he only *can* be free who is no longer anyone; impossible to be freed from oneself and also to remain oneself. The liberation from good and evil that seemed impossible and is impossible for the man whom we define by what he does or thinks and who answers to the question, "Who is that?", "It's me", is possible only who can answer at the Sundoor to the question "Who art thou?", "Thyself".[104] He who fettered himself must free himself, and that can only be done by verifying the assurance, "That art thou." It is as much for us to liberate him by knowing who we are as for him to liberate himself by knowing Who he is;[105] and that is why in the Sacrifice the sacrificer identifies himself with the victim.

Hence also the prayer, "*What* thou art, thus may I be",[106] and the eternal significance of the critical question "In *whose* departure, when I go hence, shall I be departing?",[107] i.e. in myself, or "her immortal Self " and "Leader".[108] If the right answers have been verified, if one has found the Self, and having done all that there is to be done (*kṛtakṛtya*), without any residue of potentiality (*kṛtyā*, BG.III.17),[109] the last end of our life has been presently attained.[110] It cannot be too much emphasized that freedom and immortality[111] can be, not so much "reached", as "realised" as well here and now as in any hereafter. One

MU.III.3, etc.). The operation is mechanical and servile; the operator being only free to the extent that his own will is so identified with the patron's that he becomes his own "employer" (*kārayitṛ*). "*My* service is perfect freedom."

[104]JUB.III.14, etc. Cf. my "The 'E' at Delphi", *Review of Religion*, Nov. 1941.

[105]For "ransoming Self by self ", see KB.VIII.3.

[106]TS.I.5.7.6.

[107]Pras.Up.VI.3; cf. answers in CU.III.14.4 and Kaus Up.II.14.

[108]CU.VIII.12.1; MU.III.2, VI.7. For the *hegemōn* = leader, see AA.II.6 and RV.V.50.1.

[109]But *kṛtyakṛt* (AV.IV.28.6, X.2.23) is evil-doer, where *kṛtya*, potentiality is in itself evil.

[110]AA.II.5; SA.II.4; MU.VI.30, cf.TS.I.8.1. *Kṛtyakṛta*, "all in act" corresponds to Pali *kataṁkaranīyam* in the well known "Arhat formula".

[111]*Amṛtattva* is literally "not dying", and so far as born beings, whether Gods or men are concerned, does not imply an everlasting duration but the "whole of life", i.e. "not dying" prematurely (ŚB.IX.5.1.10; PB.XXII.12.2, etc.). Thus the whole of man's life (*āyus* = *aeon*) is a *hundred* years (RV.I.89.9, II.27.10; AA.I.2.2, etc.); that of the Gods a "thousand years" or whatever this round number is taken to mean (ŚB.VIII.7.4.9, X.2.1.11, XI.1.6.6,15). So when the Gods, who were originally "mortal" obtain their "immortality" (RV.V.3.4, X.63.4; ŚB.XI-2-3-6, etc.) this is to be taken only relatively; it only means that as compared with mortal men, their life is longer (ŚB.VII.3.1.10, Śaṅkarācārya on *Brahmā Sutra* I.2.17 and II.3.7, etc.). God alone, as being "unborn", or "born only as it were", is immortal absolutely; Agni, *viśvāyus* = *pur aiōnios*, eternal fire; alone "immortal amongst mortals, God amongst gods" (RV.IV.2.1; ŚB.II.2.2.8, etc.). His timeless (*akāla*) nature is that of the "now" without duration, of which we, who can only think in terms of past and future (*bhūtam bhavyam*), have not and cannot have experience. From him all things proceed, and in him all are unified (*eko bhavanti*) at last (AA.11.3.8, etc.). There are, in other words, three orders of "not

"freed in this life" (*jīvanmukta*) "dies no more" (*na punarmriyate*).[112] "The Comprehensor of that Contemplative, ageless, undying Self, in whom naught whatsoever is wanting and who wanteth nothing, has no fear of death".[113] Having died already, he is, as the Sufi puts it, "a dead man walking".[114] Such a one no longer loves himselves or others, but is the Self in himself and in them. Death to one's self is death to "others"; and if the "dead man" seems to be "unselfish", this will not be the result of altruistic motives, but accidentally, and because he is literally un-self-ish. Liberated from himself, from all status, all duties, all rights, he has become a Mover-at-will (*kāmācārī*),[115] like the Spirit (*Vāyu, ātmā devānām*) that "moveth as it will" (*yathā vaśaṁ carati*),[116] and as St. Paul expresses it, "no longer under the law".

This is the superhuman impartiality of those who have found their Self,—"The same am I in all beings, of whom there is none I love and none I hate";[117] the freedom of those who have fulfilled the condition required of his disciples by Christ, to hate father and mother and likewise their own "life" in the world.[118] We cannot say what the freeman (*mukta*) is, but only what he is not,—*Trasumanar significar per verba non si poria!* ("he has gone beyond human limits through the word and not by action").

But this can be said that those who have not known themselves are neither now nor ever shall be free, and that "great is the destruction" of these victims of their own sensations.[119] The Brāhmaṇical autology is no more pessimistic than optimistic, but only more authoritative than any other science of which

---

dying", that of man's longevity, that of the God's aeviternity, and that of God's being without duration (On "aeviternity" cf. St. Thomas Aquinas, *Sum.Theol.* I.10.5).

The Indian texts lend themselves to no illusions: all things under the Sun are in the power of Death (ŚB.II.3.3.7); and in so far as he descends into the world, the deity himself is a "dying God"; there is no possibility of never dying in the body (ŚB.II.2.2.14, X.4.3.9; JUB.III.38.10, etc.); birth and death are inseparably connected (BG.II.27; A.IV.137; Sn. 742).

It may be observed that Gk. *athanasia* has similar values; for the "mortal immortality", cf. Plato, *Symposium* 207D-208B, and Hermes, *Lib.*XI.1.4a and *Ascl.* III.40b.

[112]ŚB.II.3.3.9; BU.I.5.2, etc., Luke 20.36, John 11.26.

[113]AV.X.8.44, cf. AA.III.2.4.

[114]*Mathnawī*, VI.723f. Also attributed to *Mathnawī* is—"Die before ye die". See also *Chuang Tzu*, Ch. 2—"burief myself", and *Angelus Silesius.*

[115]RV.IX.113.9; JUB.III.28.3; SA.VII.22; BU.II.1.17, 18;

CU.VIII.5.4, VIII.1.6 (cf.D.I.72); Taitt.Up.III.10.5 (like John X.9).

[116]RV.IX.88.3, X.168.4; cf. John III.8; *Gylfiginning*, 18.

[117]BG.IX.29.

[118]Luke XIV.26, cf. MU.VI.28 "If to son and wife and family he be attached, for such a one, no, never at all"; Sn.60—*puttaṁ ca dāram pitaram ca mātaram . . . hitvāna*; Meister Eckhart, "As long as thou still knowest who thy father and thy mother have been in time, thou art not dead with the real death" (Pfeiffer, p. 462). Cf. note 43 from 'Buddhism' section.

Phaedo 68 A, Philosopher, escapes from what he hated, namely, *sōma*, the body [*ho te diebeblento* = the body by which they had been deceived].

the truth does not depend on our wishes. It is no more pessimistic to recognize that whatever is alien to Self is a distress, than it is optimistic to recognize that where there is no "other" there is literally nothing to be feared.[120] That our Outer Man is "another" appears in the expression: "I cannot trust myself ",—but how implicitly my Self ! and "I forgot myself ". What has been called the "natural optimism" of the Upanishads is their affirmation that our consciousness of being, although invalid as an awareness of being so-and-so, is valid absolutely, and their doctrine that the Gnosis of the Immanent Deity, our Inner Man, can be realised *now.* "That *art* thou". In the words of St. Paul, *Vivo autem, jam non ego.* ("... nevertheless I live; yet not I ...". *Gal.* 2.20.)

That this is so, or that "He is" at all, cannot be demonstrated in the classroom, where only quantitative tangibles are dealt with. At the same time, it would be unscientific to deny a presupposition for which an experimental proof is possible. In the present case there is a Way[121] prescribed for those who will consent to follow it: and it is precisely at this point that we must turn from the first principles to the operation through which, rather than by which, they can be verified; in other words from the consideration of the contemplative to the consideration of the active or sacrificial life.

[119]BU.IV.4.14; CU.VII.1.6, VII.8.4, etc.

[120]BU.I.4.2.

[121]On Way or Via see *Enneads* VI and also note 66. On the pursuance of a Way, see further—

Phaedrus 253A—*ichneuontes de par heautōn aneuriskein tēn tou spheterou theou phusin euporousi* = They prosper, following the scent of their own accord, in order to discover the nature of their own god.

Enneads III.8.11—*ichnos to agathou* = trace of the good. Plato, *Laws* 728D—*ichneusai de kai helein to pantōn ariston* = to track out and choose the chief good; (which when a man has found, he should take up his abode with it during the remainder of his life).

Philebus 32D, 44D—*dei diathēreuthenai* = we must hunt down that which we are pursuing.

Plato, *Republic* 432B—"... like huntsmen, we should ... look sharp. ... but you must show me the way ... the wood is dark and perplexing; still we must push on".

Rūmī, *Mathnawī* II.160.

THE WAY OF WORKS

The Sacrifice reflects the Myth; but like all reflections, inverts it. What had been a process of generation and division becomes now one of regeneration and composition.[122] Of the two "selves" that dwell together in and depart together from this body, the first is born of woman, and the second from the sacrificial Fire, of which divine womb the man's seed is to be born again as another than he was; and until he has thus been reborn he has but the one, mortal "self".[123] To sacrifice is to be born, and it can be said, "As yet unborn, forsooth, is the man who does not sacrifice".[124] Again, when the Progenitor, our Father, "has expressed and fondly (*preṇā, sneha vaśena*) inhabits his children, he cannot come together again (*punar sambhū*) from them"[125] and so he proclaims that "They shall flourish who will build me up again (*punar ci*)[126] hence": the Gods built him up, and they flourished, and so does the sacrificer even today flourish both here and hereafter.[127] The sacrificer, in his edification of the Fire(-altar)[128] "with his whole mind, his whole self"[129]—"This Fire knows that he has come to give himself to me"[130]—is "putting together" (*saṁdhā, saṁskṛ*) at one and the same time the dismembered deity and his own separated nature: for he would be under a great delusion and merely a brute were he to hold that "He is one, and I another".[131]

The Sacrifice is something to be done; "We must do what the gods did *erst*" (in the beginning).[132] It is, in fact, often spoken of simply as "Work" (*karma*).

[122]Śaṅkarācārya, *Śataśloki* 22—*hūyate svaprabodhe Viśvam brahmaṇya bodhe jagati punaridam hūyate brahma*— "When the Self is realised, the universe is sacrificed into Brāhmaṇ; and when the Self is not realised, this Brāhmaṇ is again sacrificed into the universe". For *Birth* of the Sacrifice, see JUB.III.14.8; KB.XV.3; and *Division* of the Sacrifice, cf. TS.VI.4.2.1; RV.X.90.11-12; *Putting together* again, AB.I.18.

[123]JB.I.17: ŚB.VII.2.1.6 with VII.3.1.12; BU.II.1.11; Sn.160 and innumerable texts differentiating the two selves. The doctrine that "there are two in us" is universal, notably Indian, Islamic, Platonic, Chinese and Christian. Cf. "On Being in One's Right Mind", *Review of Religion*, VII.32f.

[124]KB.XV.3; JUB.III.14.8; ŚB.I.6.4.21, III.9.4.23; John 3.3-7.

[125]TS.V.5.2.1, cf. ŚB.I.6.3.35-6; Śaṅkarācārya, *Brahmā Sutra* II.3.46.

[126]ŚB.VI.1.2.16-21.

[127]TS.V.5.2.1. The whole creation participates in the benefits of the Sacrifice ŚB.I.5.2.4; CU.V.24.3.

[128]ŚB.X.2.4.8.

[129]ŚB.III.8.1.2, etc.

[130]ŚB.II.4.1.11, IX.5.1.53.

[131]BU.I.4.10, IV.5.7. Cf. Meister Eckhart, "Wer got minnet für sīnen got unde got an betet für sīnen got und imdā mite lāzet genügen daz ust nurals, ein augelovbic mensche" (Pfeiffer 469). "One who loves God as his God and worships God as his God, and lets God have his way (will) with him, such a one is an angelic man."

[132]ŚB.VII.2.1.4, etc.

Thus just as in Latin *operare* = *sacra facere* = *hieropoiein* (to make sacred), so in India, where the emphasis on action is so strong, to do well is to do sacred things, and only to do nothing, or what being done amiss amounts to nothing (*akṛtam*) is idle and profane.[133] How strictly analogous the operation is to any other professional work will be apparent if we remember that it is only when priests operate on behalf of others that they are to be remunerated and that when men sacrifice together on their own behalf a reception of gifts is inordinate.[134] The King as supreme Patron of the Sacrifice on behalf of the kingdom, represents the sacrificer in divinis, and is himself the type of all other sacrificers.[135]

One of the strangest controversies in the history of Orientalism turned upon the "origin of *bhakti*", as if devotion had at some given moment been a new idea and thenceforth a fashionable one. It would have been simpler to observe that the word *bhakti* means primarily a given share,[136] and therefore

[133]"Among the Tarahumares of Mexico the word *nolāvoa* means both "to work" and "to dance".—Jane Harrison, *Ancient Art and Ritual*, 1918, p. 31.

Regarding the Tarahumara Indians, Preuss writes, "Tanzen ist ihnen daher . . . - gleich arbeiten" trans: "Danemg is for them to work" in *Der ursprung der Religion und Kunst*, Globus 87, 1905, p. 336. See also Ernst Cassirer, *Language and Myth*, 1946, p. 40.

[134]TS.VII.2.10.2. At such a "seance" the Self (Spirit) is the guerdon and it is in as much as the sacrificers obtain the Self as their reward that they go to heaven (*ātma-dakṣinaṁ vai sattram, ātmānam eva nītvā suvargaṁ lokam yanti*, TS.VII.4.9.1, cf.PB.IV.9.19). KB.XV.1 "The sattra has the Self as Dakṣiṇā (from *dakṣayati*, 'empowers') . . . 'Here let me take my Self as *dakṣiṇā* for fair fame, for the world of heaven, for Immortality'".

CU.III.17.4 where the whole of life is sacrificially interpreted—.

ŚB.IX.5.2.12-16 condemns sacrificial operation for others, than oneself.

Otherwise *dakṣiṇā* is due to priests because in the sacrifice they as spiritual fathers, make the sacrificer to be born again of the divine womb.

St. Augustine, *De Civitas Dei* X.VI. "A true sacrifice is every work which brings about that we may be united to God in holy association".

[135]Demand to the Christian martyrs before condemnation: *Fac pro salute Imperatoris* = "Make sacrifice for the Emperor's wellbeing", and *Hoc facita in meam commemorationem*, may mean—"Make this sacrifice in memory of me".

[136]The *bhakta* is one who gives his share to another, which giving, especially of oneself, implies love (as in Mīrā Bāi's lines on p. 28).

For *bhakti* as "participation", refer Betty Heimann, *Facets of Indian Thought*, London, 1964, p. 86.

AV.20. "pausiṣṭa" (see JAOS XV, Proceedings, p. v)

skandayāga, bhaktvā devam (Skandakumura) *visarjayet*.

Note: *bhakṣ* to consume, and *bhiks* desiderative of *bhaj* = to share, distribute, apportion; Greek *phagein* = to eat, devour; Latin *fagus* = beech tree, book.

For a fuller treatment of the concept of *bhakti* as sacrifice, see *Spiritual Authority and Temporal Power*. . . note 75 in the edition of 1993. Yet other sources: *Liturgical Homilies of Narsai* XXI, p. 55—"The silver of His word He has placed in their hands by way of inducement, that they may trade with each (and gain) possessions of the spiritual life". And Rūmī, *Shams-i-Tabrīz* Ode 45.11—"Where is the fortunate merchant whose destiny Jupiter controls, that I (God) may eagerly trade with him and buy his wares?"

St. Matthew, V.12—Rejoice for great is your reward in heaven.

also the devotion or love that all liberality presupposes; and so that in as much as one "gives God his share (*bhāgam*), i.e. sacrifices, one is his *bhakta*".[137] Thus in the hymn, "If thou lovest me".[138] It has often been pointed out that the Sacrifice was thought of as a commerce between gods and men:[139] but not often realised that by introducing into traditional conceptions of trade, notions derived from our own internecine commercial transactions, we have falsified our understanding of the original sense of such a commerce, which was actually more of the *potlatsh* type, a competition in giving, than like our competitions in taking. The sacrificer knows that for whatever he gives he will receive full measure in return; or rather, fuller measure, for whereas his own treasury is limited, the other party's is inexhaustible.[140] "He is the Imperishable (-syllable, Aum), for he pours forth to all these beings, and because there is none can pour forth beyond him".[141] God gives as much as we can take of him, and that depends on how much of "ourselves" we have given up. Feudal

[137]BU.VI.3.1—*tebhyoham bhāgadheyam juhomi* = "to all those gods . . . I offer their share".

RV.II.5.7—*aram vanemā rarimā vayam*; saying *sambhajema . . . dademahi.* Griffith's trans.: "We have bestowed . . . let us obtain".

ŚB.II.3.1.19—*tasmād devāh santi . . .* (other beings) *anvābhaktāh.* Thereby the gods are allowed to share in the sacrifice with other participants.

PB.VI.7—*bhāgadheyena . . .* on winning favour of the gods . . .*vāc* complains of being *abhāga.*

[138]ŚB.I.9.3.8—" . . . He who sacrifices assuredly gratifies the gods. In gratifying the gods by that sacrifice . . . he acquires a share among them; and having acquired a share among them, he goes to them".

St. Thomas Aquinas, *Supp.* 95.1 2—"Love is the cause of all giving".

Plato, *Euthyphro* 14D—"Piety is a science of asking and giving? . . . an art which gods and men have of doing business with one another?"

Rūmī, *Mathnawī* VI.885—"Trade with God".

[139]TS.I.8.4.1; AV.III.15.5.6.

[140]*Bhaj,* the root in *bhakti,* etc., and in bhikṣu (the religious mendicant who expects to be fed) is nearly synonymous with *sev, upacār, therapeuō* (= to attend on); and implies a service or attendance upon any worthy recipient, human or divine. In the older contexts it is usually the Deity who participates such boons as life or light to others, and is therefor called Bhaga or Bhagavat, "Dispenser", that which is given being a "participation" or "dispensation" (*bhāgam*). But already in RV.VIII.100.1, Indra is manifestly Agni's *bhakta,* and this is the natural relation of the Regnum to the Sacerdotium; and in RV.X.51.8 those whom Agni calls upon to "give me my share" (*haviṣo dattabhāgam*) are to be his *bhaktas.* Every sacrifice involves the giving of the share (*bhāgam*) that is due to the recipient, and is in this sense a devotion, ultimately of the sacrificer himself, the devotee; this implies love, because love is the cause of all giving, but it remains that bhakti can be more literally translated by "participation" in some contexts and by "devotion" in others, than by "love", for which the word is *prema.*

[141]AA.II.2.2. "He", the immanent Breath (*prāṇa*), Vāmadeva, Indra. The point is that the transcendental Syllable (*akṣara* = Aum) is the source of all uttered sounds (cf. CU.II.23.3; BG.X.25), itself remaining inexhaustible (*akṣara*),—pouring forth but never poured out.

loyalties rather than business obligations are implied words of the hymns, "Thou art ours and we art thine"; "Let us, O Varuṇa, be thine own dearly beloved" and "Thine may we be for thee to give us treasure".[142] These are the relations of thane to earl and vassal to overlord, not of money-changers. The language of commerce survives even in such late and profoundly devotional hymns as Mīrā Bāi's

Kānh have I bought. The price he asked, I gave.
Some cry, "Tis great", and others jeer, " 'Tis small"
I gave in full, weighed to the utmost grain,
My love, my life, my soul, my all.[143]

If we also remember, what will shortly appear, that the sacrificial life is the active life, it will be seen that the connection of action with devotion is implicit in the very concept of operation; and that whatever is done perfectly must have been done lovingly, and whatever ill done, done carelessly.

The Sacrifice, like the words of the liturgy indispensable to it, must be understood (erlebt) if it is to be completely effective. The merely physical acts may, like any other labour, secure temporal advantages. Its uninterrupted celebration maintains, in fact, the endless "stream of wealth" (*vasor dhārā*) that falls from heaven as the fertilising rain, passes through plants and animals, becomes our food, and is returned to heaven in the smoke of the Burnt-offering; that rain and this smoke are the wedding gifts in the sacred marriage of Sky and Earth, Sacerdotium and Regnum, that is implied by the

[142]RV.VIII.92.32, VIII.54.8; V.85.8 and VII.19.7, Indra; RV.II.11.1; AA.II.1.4.18. Cf. Plato, *Phaedo*, 62B,D.

[143]As for Krishna and the Gopis, let me say with Plotinus that "it is because Love is of the Psyche's very nature that we have the constant yoking of Eros with the Psyches in the pictures and the myths' (*Enneads* 6.6.9), and let us also bear in mind the saying of the Puritan Platonist Peter Sterry that "the Lord Jesus hath his concubines, his Queenes, his Virgines . . . Saints unmarried to any Forme, who keep themselves single for the immediate imbraces of their Love".

Other definitions of Bhakti:

By Śāṅkarācārya in *Vivekachudāmaṇi*—32, 33 *svasvarūpānusandhānam* or *svātma-tattvānusandhānam.*

By Nārada, *Bhaktisūtras*-2 *sā tvasmin paramapremarūpa.*

By Śāndilya, *Śāṅdilyabhaktisūtra sāparamānuraktir īśvare.* "Commerce" became a natural symbol of the intentions of man with God just because "commerce" had originally been "une pratique perfectionnée de l'éxchanges des cadeaux".—(W.C. Hardy: *L'art des Iles Marquises*, 1938)—a hard mouthful for us to swallow, for whom trade is synonymous with exploitation!

Roman Breviary adfin: at the end: that at one and the same time it may support our mortal life and obtain for us everlasting happiness.

The archetype of human-divine commerce is prescribed by the BG.III.10-11— " . . . cherishing one another, ye shall gain the highest good".

whole operation.[144] But more than the mere acts is required if their ultimate purpose, of which the acts are only the symbols, is to be realised. It is explicit that "neither by action nor by sacrifices can He be reached" (*nakiṣṭaṁ karmaṇā naśad—na yajñaiḥ*),[145] whom to know is our highest good:[146] and at the same time repeatedly affirmed that the Sacrifice is performed, not merely aloud and visibly, but also "intellectually" (*manasā*),[147] i.e. silently and invisibly, within you. In other words, the practise is only the external support and demonstration of the theory. The distinction is drawn accordingly between the true self-sacrificer (*sadyājī, satisad, ātmayājī*) and the one who is merely present at a sacrifice (*sattrasad*) and expects the deity to do all the real work (*devayājī*).[148] It is even stated in so many words that "Whoever, being a Comprehensor thereof performs the good work, or is simply a Comprehensor (without actually performing any rite), puts together again the dismembered deity, whole and complete";[149] it is by gnosis and not by works that that world is attainable.[150] Nor can it be overlooked that the rite, in which the sacrificer's last end is prefigured, is an exercise in dying, and therefore a dangerous undertaking[151] in which the sacrificer might actually lose his life prematurely; but "the Comprehensor passes on from one duty to another, as from one stream into another, or from one refuge to another, to obtain his weal, the heavenworld".[152]

We cannot describe in detail the "wilds and realms" of the Sacrifice, and shall only consider that most significant part of the Burnt-offering (*agnihotra*) in which the Soma oblation is poured into the Fire as into God's mouth. What is Soma? Exoterically, an intoxicating drink, extracted from the juicy parts of various plants and mixed with milk and honey and filtered, and corresponding to the mead or wine or blood of other traditions. This juice, however, is not itself Soma until "by means of the priest, the initiation and the formulae", and "by faith" it has been made to be Soma, transubstantially;[153] and "Though men fancy when they crush the plant that they are drinking of very Soma, of him the Brāhmaṇas understand by 'Soma' none tastes who dwells on earth".[154] The plants made use of are not the real Soma plant, which grows in the rocks and mountains (*giri, aśman, adri*), in which it is embodied.[155]

[144] *Vasor dhārā*, TS.V.4.8.1, V.7.3.2; ŚB.IX.3.2.3; AA.II.1.2, III.1.2; MU.VI.37; BG.III.10.f., etc. Wedding gifts, PB.VII.10; AB.IV.27; JB.1.145; ŚB.I.8.3.12, etc.

[145] RV.VIII.70.3; AA.III.2.6; ŚB.X.5.4.16 and A.B. Keith in AA., p. 257, note 10.

[146] AA.II.2.3; Kaus.Up.III.1.

[147] RV.passim; cf. TS.II.5.11.4-5; BU.IV.4.19; KB.XXVI.6.

[148] ŚB.XI.2.6.13,14; ŚB.VIII.6.1.10; MU.VI.9. See also my "Ātmayajña" in HJAS, 6, 1942.

[149] ŚB.X.4.3.24, etc.

[150] ŚB.X.5.4.16; an echo of RV.VIII.70.3.

[151] ŚB.IX.1.1.32-3—descent after ascent.

[152] ŚB.XII.2.3.12.

[153] AB.VII.31; ŚB.III.4.3.13, XII.7.3.11.

[154] RV.X.8.34.

[155] RV.V.43.4; ŚB.III.4.3.13; ŚB.XII.3.2.12; RV.IX.113.1-11; RV.VIII.48.3.

The "pacification" or slaying of King Soma, the God, is rightly called the Supreme Oblation. Yet it is not Soma himself, "but only his evil" that is killed:[156] it is, actually in prepartion for his enthronement and sovereignty that Soma is purified;[157] and this is a pattern followed in coronation rites (*rājasūya*) and descriptive of the soul's preparation for her own autonomy (*svarāj*). For it must never be forgotten that "Soma was the Dragon" and is sacrificially extracted from the Dragon's body just as the living sap (*rasa*) is extracted from a decorticated tree. It is in agreement with the rule that the "Suns are Serpents" that have cast and abandoned their dead reptilian skins[158] that Soma's procession is described: "Even as the Serpent from his inveterated skin, so (from the bruised shoots) streams the golden Soma-jet, like a sportive steed".[159] In just the same way the procession and liberation of our immortal Self from its psycho-physical sheaths (*kośa*; Gk. *endumata* = garments) is a shaking off of bodies,[160] or as one draws a reed from its sheath, or an arrow from its quiver to find its mark, or as a snake skin is sloughed; "even as the serpent casts its skin, so does one cast off all his evil".[161]

We can now more easily understand the identification of Soma juice with the Water of Life, that of our composite elemental soul (*bhūtātman*) with the Soma shoots from which the regal elixir is to be extracted,[162] and how and by whom "what the Brāhmaṇas mean by Soma" is consumed in our hearts (*hṛtsu*).[163] It is the life-blood of the draconian soul that its harnessed powers now offer to their Overlord.[164] The sacrificer makes Burnt-offering of what is

---

It is only in Yama's realm, in the otherworld, third heaven, that Soma himself can be partaken of; nevertheless the sacrificer, ritually and analogically "drinketh of Soma in symposium with the Gods" (*sadhamādam devaiḥ somam pibati*), and can say "we have drunk Soma, we have become immortal, we have seen the Light, we have found the Gods; what can the enmity, what the treachery of a mortal do unto us, O thou Immortal"?

TS.I.7.10; TS.III.2.5—"We have drunk the Soma, we have become immortal. . . ."

TS.II.5.5.5—*sadhamādam devaiḥ somam pibati* see picture of Sumerian Seals.

The Eucharistic character of the ritual is obvious. Cf. AB.I.22 "May we eat of thee, O God Gharma" and *Math.* XXVI.26—" . . . Take, eat; this is my body".

[156] ŚB.III.9.4.17, 18.

[157] ŚB.III.3.2.6.

[158] PB.XXV.15.4.

[159] RV.IX.86.44.

[160] TS.VII.4.9; PB.IV.9.19-22; JUB.I.15.3.f., III.30.2; CU.VIII.13, Cf. BU.III.7.3.f., CU.VIII.12.1. Attainment of immortality in the body is impossible (ŚB.X.4.3.9; JUB.III.38.10, etc.). Cf. *Phaedo*, 67C "Katharsis (= *śuddha karaṇa*) is the separation of the soul from the body, as far as that is possible".

[161] ŚB.II.5.2.47; BU.IV.4.7, and passim.

[162] MU.III.3f.

[163] RV.I.168.3, I.179.5, cf. RV.X.107.9 (*antaḥpeyam*).

[164] Cf. Philo, LA.II.56, "to pour out as a libation the blood of the soul and to offer as incense the whole mind to God our Saviour and Benefactor". *Hamadhānī*—"To meet with Me and behold My beauty is what I give in return for the blood of My Lovers" (see BSOS.V.914).

his and what he is, and is emptied out of himself,[165] becoming a God. When the rite is relinquished he returns to himself, from the real to the unreal.[166] But although in thus returning he says "Now I am who I am", the very statement shows that he knows that this is not really, but only temporarily true. He has been born again of the Sacrifice, and is not really deceived. "Having slain his own Dragon"[167] he is no longer really anyone; the work has been done, once and for all; he has come to the end of the road and end of the world, "where Heaven and Earth embrace", and may thereafter "work" or "play" as he will; it is to him that the words are spoken, *Lo tuo piacere omai prende per duce—per ch'io te sopra te corono e mitrio.*[168]

We who were at war with ourselves are now reintegrated and self-composed: the rebel has been tamed (*dānta*) and pacified (*śānta*), and where there had been a conflict of wills there is now unanimity.[169] We can only very briefly allude to another and very significant aspect of the Sacrifice that has been made by pointing out that the reconciliation of conflicting powers for which

[165]ŚB.III.8.1.2; TS.I.7.5.2. As it was in the beginning, RV.X.90.5; ŚB.III.9.1.2.

[166]The Gods are true, or real (*satyam*), men false or unreal (*amṛtam*), AB.1.6; ŚB.I.1.1.4, III.9.4.1, etc. [universals are real, particulars unreal]. The initiated sacrificer has fallen away from this world and is temporarily a God, Agni or Indra (ŚB.III.3.3.10; ŚB.VI.4.4.10 with *ṛtam* = *agni*, and *satyam* = deus, agni standing for both). TS.V.1.6.7 *ujam vai ṛtam, asau satyam.* Cf. Heres 84—the priest is "not a man" while he is in the Holy of Holies. If no provision were made for the sacrificer's return to the world of men, he would be liable to die prematurely (TS.I.7.6.6, etc.). The redescent is therefore provided for (TS.V.I.3.10.4; PB.XVIII.10.10; AB.IV.21); and it is in returning to the human world of unreality or false hood and becoming this man so-and-so once more that he says "Now I am who I am" (*aham ya evāsmi so'smi,* ŚB.I.9.3.23; AB.VII.24; S.III.25,26); a tragic confession that he is "once again conscious of a more limited, even a bodily and earthly life" (Macdonald, *Phantastes,* 1858, p. 317). For there can be no greater sorrow than to reflect that we still are what we are (*Cloud of Unknowing,* Ch. 44).

Shams-i-Tabriz, p. 233—"There is no crime worse than thy being".

[167]TS.II.5.4.5.

[168]Dante, *Purgatorio,* XXVII-131, 142—"Thou hast o'ercome the steeper way, O'ercome the straiter. . . . —I invest thee then With crown and mitre, sovereign o'er thyself ".

[169]BG.VI.7, *Jitātmanah praśāntasya paramātmā samāhitaḥ,*—"The Supreme Self of the individual-self is 'composed' (*samahitaḥ* ='in *samadhi*') when the latter has been conquered and pacified". Observe that to "pacify" is literally to give the quietus. Śānti, "peace", is not for any self that will not die. The root, *śam,* is present also in *śamayitṛ,* the "butcher" who "quiets" the sacrificial victim in the external ritual (RV.V.43.3; ŚB.III.8.3.4, etc.); the sacrificer "quenches" (*śamayati*) the fire of Varuṇa's wrath (TS.V.1.6; ŚB.IX.1.2.1); within you, it is the higher Self that "pacifies" the individual self, quenches its fire. Whoever would be "at peace with himself" must have died to himself. Cf. Dhammapada 103-5—*ekaṁ ca jeyya attānaṁ sa ve saṅgāma-juttamo . . . attā ha ve! jitam . . . n'eva devo apajitam kayivā . . . bhāvil'attānam.* He who wins this battle (psychomachy, jihad) is the true conqueror (*jīna*). Cf. Kashpal Mahsab, p. 364 on jihad. *Republic,* 556E; *Gorgias,* 482C; *Timaeus* 47D; and HJAS. VI.389, 1942 ("On Peace").

the Sacrifice continually provides is also their marriage. There are more ways than one of "killing" a Dragon; and the Dragon-slayer's bolt (*vajra*) being in fact a shaft of light, and "light the progenitive power", its signification is not only military, but also phallic.[170] It is the battle of love that has been won when the Dragon "expires". Soma as Dragon is identified with the Moon; as Elixir the Moon becomes the food of the Sun, by whom she is swallowed up[171] on the nights of their cohabitation (*amāvāsya*), and "what is eaten is called by the eater's name and not its own";[172] in other words, ingestion implies assimilation. In Meister Eckhart's words, "There the soul unites with God, as food with man, which turns in eye to eye, in ear to ear; so does the soul in God turn into God"; for "what absorbs me, that I am, rather than mine own self".[173] Just as the Sun swallows up the Dawn, or devours the Moon, visibly and outwardly, daily and monthly, such is the "divine marriage" that is consummated within you when the solar and lunar Persons of the right and left eyes, Eros and Psyche, Death and the Lady, enter into the cave of the heart and are united there, just as a man and woman are united in human wedlock, and that is their "supreme beautitude".[174] In that rapt synthesis (*samādhi*) the Self has recovered its primordial condition, "as of a man and a woman closely embraced",[175] and without awareness of any distinction of a within from a without.[176] "That Self art thou."

No wonder, then, that we find it said that "If one sacrifices, knowing not this interior Burnt-offering, it is as if he pushed aside the brands and made oblation in the ashes";[177] that this is not a rite to be performed only at fixed seasons, but on every one of the thirty six thousand days of one's whole life of a hundred years;[178] and that for the Comprehensor of this, all the powers of the soul incessantly build up his Fire even while he is asleep.[179]

[170]Cf. RV.I.32.5 *vajreṇa* = II.11.5 *vīryeṇa* as in Manu I.8 *vīryam/bījam avāsṛjat*, and in the sense of RV.X.95.4 *śnathita vaitasena.* On the *fier baiser*, Disenchantment by a Kiss, see W.H. Schofield, *Studies on the Libeaus Desconus*, 1895, 199ff., and my "The Loathly Bride", *Speculum* XX-4 [Coomaraswamy, 1: Selected Papers, Bolingen, PUP, 1977, pp. 353-70]. See also Kratislaw, *Sixty Folk Tales*, p. 305.

[171]ŚB.I.6-4.19 *grasitvā.*

[172]ŚB.X.6.2.1.

[173]"Whatever is received into anything is therein after the mode of the recipient"—St. Thomas Aquinas, *Supp.* 92-1. Meister Eckhart, Evans'trans.I.287,380. Our highest good is thus to be devoured by "Noster Deus ignis consumens". Cf. *Speculum*, XI, 1936, pp. 332, 333 and, further, Dante, *Paradiso* XXVI.51, "How many are the fangs, with which this love, Is grappled to thy soul". His kiss, who is both Love and Death, awakens us to becoming here, and his love-bite to being there. Cf. my "Sunkiss" in JAOS.60, 1940.

[174]ŚB.X.5.2.11,12.

[175]ŚB.I.4.3.

[176]BU.IV.3.21.

[177]SA.X; Cf. ŚB.II.2.4.7,8; Ṁ.1.77; CU.V.24; ŚB.I.5.2.4, II.3.1.20 and *Nirukta* 10.26, 27 in praise of Viśvakarman.

[178]ŚB.X.5.3.3; AA.11.3.8.

[179]ŚB.X.5.3.12.

This conception of the Sacrifice as an incessant operation (continuity ~ Tau) and the sum of man's duty finds its completion in a series of texts in which each and every function of the active life, down to our very breathing, eating, drinking and dalliance is sacramentally interpreted and death is nothing but the final catharsis.[180] And that is, finally, the famous "Way of Works" (*karma mārga*) of the Bhagavad Gītā, where to fulfil one's own vocation, determined by one's own nature (*svakarma, svabhāvatas* = *to heautou prattein, kata phusin* = to attend to his own practice, according to nature), with self-referent motives, is the way of perfection (*siddhi*). We have come full circle, not in an "evolution of sought" but in our own understanding, from the position that the perfect celebration of rites is our task, to the position that the perfect performance of our tasks, whatever they may be, is itself the celebration of the rite. Sacrifice, thus understood, is no longer a matter of doing specifically sacred things only on particular occasions, but of sacrificing (*making sacred*) all we do and all we are; a matter of the sanctification of whatever is done naturally, by a reduction of all activities to their principles. We say "naturally" advisedly, intending to imply that whatever is done naturally may be either sacred or profane according to our own degree of awareness, but that whatever is done *un*naturally is essentially and irrevocably profane.

[180] ŚB.IX.5.1.42—Oblations to Viśvakarman through *agnicayana* include all sacrificial rites (*viśvāni karmāni*).

THE SOCIAL ORDER

Ethics, whether as prudence or as art, is nothing but the scientific application of doctrinal norms to contingent problems; right doing or making are matters not only of the will, but primarily of conscience or awareness, a choice being only possible as between obedience or rebellion. Actions, in other words, are in order or inordinate in precisely the same way that iconography may be correct or incorrect, formal or informal.[181] Error is failure to hit the mark, and is to be expected in all who act instinctively, to please themselves. Skill (*kauśalya* = Gr. *sophia*), is virtue, whether in doing or in making: a matter needing emphasis only because it has now been generally overlooked that there can be artistic as well as moral sin. "Yoga is skill in works."[182]

[181]In fact, just as the forms of images are prescribed in the Śilpaśāstras, so those of action are prescribed in the Dharmaśāstras. Art and prudence are both equally sciences, differing from pure metaphysics only in the fact of their application to *factibilia* and *agibilia*. The fact that there is an application to contingent problems introduces an element of contingency into the laws themselves, which are not identical for all castes nor in all ages. In this sense, the tradition is adaptable to changing conditions always, provided that the solutions are derived directly from the first principles, which never change. In other words, while there can be a modification of laws only those laws that can be reduced to the Eternal Law can ever be called correct. There is, in the same way, necessarily and rightly, an application of pure metaphysics to the variety of religions that correspond to the variety of human needs, each of which religions, will be "the true religion" to the extent that it reflects the eternal principles. In saying this we distinguish between metaphysics and "philosophy" and are not suggesting that any systematic or natural philosophy can presume to the validity of the theology that Aristotle ranks above all other sciences (*Metaphysics*, I.2.12f., VI.1.10f.).

[182]"*Yogaḥ karmasu kauśalam*", BG.II.50; also "Yoga is the resignation (*saṁnyāsa*) of works", BG.VI.2. *Saṁnyāsa* is re-numeration or con-signment of works to their real author. In other words, *yoga* does not mean doing less or more than enough, nor doing nothing at all, but doing without attachment to the fruit of works, taking no thought for the morrow. "He sees indeed, who sees inaction in action, and action in inaction", BG.IV.18 and passim). This is the Chinese doctrine of *wei wu wei*.

Yoga is literally and etymologically a "yoking", as of horses; and in this connection it will not be overlooked that in India, as in Greek psychology, the "horses" of the bodily vehicle are the sensitive powers by which it is drawn this way or that, for good or evil, or to its ultimate goal if the horses are controlled by the driver to whom they are yoked by the reins. The individuality is the team, the Inner Controller or Inner Man the rider. The ego or man then, "yokes himself like an understanding horse"(RV.V.46.1).

As a physical and mental discipline, Yoga is Contemplation, *dhārana, dhyāna* and *samādhi* corresponding to Christian *consideratio, contemplatio* and *excessus* or *raptus*. In its consummation and total significance, *yoga* implies the reduction of separated

Where there is agreement as to the nature of man's last end, and that the Way by which the present and the paramount ends of life can be realised is that of sacrificial operation, it is evident that the form of society will be determined by the requirements of the Sacrifice; and that order (*yathārthatā*) and impartiality (*samadṛṣṭi*) will mean that everyman shall be enabled to become, and by no misdirection prevented from becoming, what he has it in him to become. We have seen that it is to those who maintain the Sacrifice that the promise is made that they shall flourish. Now the Sacrifice, performed in divinis by the All-worker (*Viśvakarman*), as imitated here demands a cooperation of all the arts (*viśva karmāṇi*),[183] for example, those of music, architecture, carpentry, husbandry and that of warfare to protect the operation. The politics of the heavenly, social and individual communities are governed by one and the same law. The pattern of the heavenly politics is revealed in scripture and reflected in the constitution of the autonomous state and that of the man who governs himself.

In this man, in whom the sacramental life is complete, there is a hierarchy of sacerdotal, royal and administrative powers, and a fourth class consisting of the physical organs of sense and action, that handle the raw material or "food" to be prepared for all; and it is clear that if the organism is to flourish, which is impossible if divided against itself, that the sacerdotal, royal and administrative powers, in their order of rank, must be the "masters", and the workers in raw materials their "servants". It is in precisely the same way that the functional hierarchy of the realm is determined by the requirements of the Sacrifice on which its prosperity depends. The castes are literally "born of the Sacrifice".[184] In the sacramental order there is a need and a place for

---

things to their unitary principle, and thus what is sometimes called "mystical union"; but it must be clearly realised that *yoga* differs from "mystical experience" in being, not a passive, but an active and controlled procedure. The perfected *yogi* can pass from one state of being to another at will, as for example, the Buddha, M.I.249.

Every Hindu is to some extent a practitioner of Yoga, and just what this implies is admirably stated in Plato, *Republic* 571Df., eis *sunnoian autos auto aphichomenos* = collecting himself in meditation.

When, however, it becomes a question of more intensive contemplation, and the intention is to scale the uttermost heights, the practitioner must be prepared by suitable physical exercises, and must especially have acquired a perfectly balanced control and awareness of the whole process of breathing, before he proceeds to any mental exercises; nor can any of these exercises be safely undertaken without the guidance of a master. Some idea of the nature of the first steps, by which the vagrant stream of thought is arrested and brought under control, will be gained if the attempt is made to think of some one thing, no matter what, for so long a period even as ten seconds; it will be found with surprise, and perhaps embarrassment, that even this cannot be done without much practice.

[183]ŚB.IX.5.1.42 In the same way that the Christian Sacrifice demands the collaboration of all the arts. See note 180.

[184]The best discussion of this will be found in A.M. Hocart, *Les Castes*, Paris, 1939.

all men's work: and there is no more significant consequence of the principle, Work is Sacrifice, than the fact that under these conditions, and remote as this may be from our secular ways of thinking, every function, from that of the priest and the king down to that of the potter and scavenger, is literally a priesthood and every operation a ministerial rite. In each of these spheres, moreover, we meet with "professional ethics". The caste system differs from the industrial "division of labor", with its "fractioning of human faculty", in that it presupposes differences in kinds of responsibility but not in degrees of responsibility; and it is just because an organisation of functions such as this, with its mutual loyalties and duties, is absolutely incompatible with our competitive industrialism, that the monarchic, feudal and caste system is always painted in such dark colours by the sociologist, whose thinking is determined more by his actual environment than it is by a deduction from first principles.[185]

That capacities and corresponding vocations are hereditary necessarily follows from the doctrine of progenitive rebirth: every man's son is by nativity qualified and predestined to assume his father's "character" and take his place in the world; it is for this that he is initiated into his father's profession and finally confirmed in it by the deathbed rites of transmission, after which, should the father survive, the son becomes the head of the family.[186] In replacing his father, the son frees him from the functional responsibility that he bore in this life, at the same time that a continuation of the sacrificial services is provided for.[187] And by the same token, the family line comes to an

[185]Sir George Birdwood remarks in his *Sva*, 1915, pp. 83-4: "The enactments embodied in the Code of Manu, and cognate law books of the Hindus, have achieved this consummation from before the foundations of Athens and Rome . . . we trace there the bright outlines of a self-contained, self-dependent, symmetrical, and perfectly harmonious industrial economy, deeply rooted in the popular conviction of its divine character, and protected, through every political and commercial vicissitude, by the absolute power and marvellous wisdom and tact of the Brāhmaṇical priesthood. Such an ideal social order we should have held impossible of realisation, but that it continues to exist, and to afford us, in the yet living results of its daily operation in India, a proof of the superiority, in so many unsuspected ways, of the hieratic civilization of antiquity over the secular, joyless, inane, and self-destructive modern civilization of the West."

[186]One reason for the current decline of birth rate is the loss of a sense of responsibility to society in this respect, which must be a loss of the concept of vocation, metier, ministerium. Each responsibility implies the other.

[187]AA.II.4.5; Ait.Up.IV.4—"For the perpetuation of these worlds; for thus are these worlds perpetuated. That is his being born again. This self of his is put in his place for the doing of holy works [ŚB.X.4.3.9, I.9.3.21, VIII.6.1.10; BU.I.5.17]. That other Self of his, having done what there was to be done, and reached his age departs (from this world). That is his third birth." Cf. JUB.III.9.6; MU.VI.30 RV.VI.70.3 *pra prajābhir jāyate dharmaṇas pari* RV.IX.97.30 *pitu(na) putraḥ kratubhir* (Sāyaṇa-*karmabhir*) *yatāna* = as a son persevering in sacrificial rites secures his father's welfare. Similarly ŚB.I.8.1.31

end, not for want of descendants (since this can be remedied by adoption) but whenever the family vocation and tradition is abandoned. In the same way a total confusion of castes is the death of a society, nothing but a mob remaining where a man can change his profession at will, as though it had been something altogether independent of his own nature. It is, in fact, thus that traditional societies are murdered and their culture destroyed by contact with industrial and proletarian civilisations. The orthodox Eastern estimate of Western civilisation can be fairly stated in Mathew Arnold's words:

> The East bow'd low before the West
> In patient, deep disdain.

It must be remembered, however, that contrasts of this kind can be drawn only as between the still orthodox East and the modern West, and would not have held good in the thirteenth century.

The social order is designated, by its integration of functions, to provide at the same time for a common prosperity and to enable every member of society to realise his own perfection. In the sense that "religion" is to be identified with the "law" and distinguished from the "spirit", Hindu religion is strictly speaking an obedience; and that this is so appears clearly in the fact that a man is considered to be a Hindu in good standing, not by what he believes but by what he does; or in other words, by his "skill" in well doing under the law.

For if there is no liberation by works, it is evident that the practical part of the social order, however faithfully fulfilled, can no more than any other rite, or than the affirmative theology, be regarded as anything more than a means to an end beyond itself. There always remains a last step, in which the ritual is abandoned and the relative truths of theology denied. As it was by the knowledge of good and evil that man fell from his first high estate, so it must be from the knowledge of good and evil, from the moral law, that he must be delivered at last. However far one may have gone, there remains a last step to be taken, involving a dissolution of all former values. A church or society (religion or culture)—the Hindu would make no distinction—that does not

---

tasmāt prajottarā devayajyā = "future worship of the gods means offspring". The inheritance of vocations provides for the continuity of divine service. Caste and vocation is hereditary; one should not relinquish the work to which one is born—*sahajamkarma . . . na tyajet*, BG.XVIII.48. Supported by *Ecclesiasticus* 38:34—"But they will maintain the fabric of the world, And in the handiwork of their craft is their prayer". From the same point of view in Plato, *Laws* 773Ef., "Concerning marriage . . . it is decreed that we should adhere to the ever-productive nature by providing servants of God in our own stead; and this we do by always leaving behind us children's children". Supported by Sir Peter Renouf in his *Religion of Egypt*, p.147—"Let a child remain in my place for ever and ever keeping alive the name of my house." Similarly, ŚB.I.8.1.31 *Tasmāt prajottarā devayajnā*. Cf. ŚB VIII.6.1.13, BV 15.17, Dante's *Paradiso* (no reference given); Aesch.Cho. 256f.; Philo, *De Conf.* 96 and *De Dec.* 199.

provide a way of escape from its own regimen, and will not let its people go, is defeating its own ultimate purpose.[188]

It is precisely for this last step that provision is made in the last of what are called the "Four Stages" (*āśramas*) of life.[189] The term itself implies that every man is a pilgrim (śramaṇa, asketes), whose only motto is to "keep on going" (caraiva). The first of these stages is that of student-discipleship; the second that of marriage and occupational activity, with all its responsibilities and rights; the third is one of retreat and comparative poverty; the fourth a condition of total renunciation (*sannyāsa*).[190] It will be seen that whereas in a secular society a man looks forward to an old age of comfort and economic independence, in this sacramental order (consignment) he looks forward to becoming independent of economics and indifferent to comfort and discomfort. I recall the figure of one of the most magnificent men: having been a householder of almost fabulous wealth, he was now at the age of seventy-eight in the third stage, living alone in a log cabin and doing his own cooking and washing with his own hands the only two garments he possessed. In two years more he would have abandoned all this semi-luxury to become a religious mendicant, without any possessions whatever but a loin cloth and a begging bowl in which to receive scraps of food freely given by others still in the second stage of life.

This fourth stage of life may also be entered upon at any time, if and only if, a man be ripe for it and the call be irresistible. Those who thus abandon the household life and adopt the homeless are variously known as renouncers, wanderers or marksmen (*sannyāsī, pravrājaka, sādhu*)[191] and as Yogis. It

[188]On Law and Liberty cf. St. Augustine, De spiritu et littera. It is by the Spiritual Power that the Temporal power is freed from its bondage ("...verily by the holy power Brāhman, he [Bṛhaspati] frees him [Indra] from the bond that fetters him". TS.II.4.13) Cf. AB.VII.13.

[189]MU.IV.4. See also Śāṅkarācārya, *Brahmā Sutra,* ŚBE. Vol. XXXVIII, Index, s.v. "Stages of life (*āśrama*)". The first three lead to heavenly states of being, only the fourth, which may be entered upon at any time, to an absolute immortality in God.

On the fourth *āśrama* cf. Plato, "But with the advance of age, when the soul begins to attain maturity . . . they should do nothing but (consider all time and all being), unless as a by-work, if they are to lead a blessed life and when they finish crown the life they have led (here) with a corresponding lot there . . . when they reach that life in which they will be born again" (*Republic,* 498C, D with 486 A). With a "mortified" life, a true philosophy is an *ars moriendi,* art of dying, *videhamukti* (*Phaedo,* 61, 64, 67).

[190]While distinguishing √*tyaj, tyāga* = forsaking from *saṁnyāsa* = relinquishing, see the several implications of *saṁnyāsa* and *karma* in BG.V.1-2, III.30, VI.2, V.10, II.50, III.27, V.8, IX.27, V.13.

[191]For references to *pravraj* = to go into exile, to renounce all worldly attachments, to enter on the fourth stage in life, see BU.IV.4.22, IV.5.2.

On *vraj,* to be banished, etc., cf. Philo, *Raem.* 117—"not the discredited flight of the outcast, but a flight of one banished from evil to salvation, a banishment which may be truly held to be better than a recall". Cf. Philo, *De Abr.* and *De Migr.*

happens even today that men of the highest rank, achievement and wealth "change their lives" (*anyad vṛttam upākarisyan*, BU.IV.5.1) in this way; this is literally a dying to the world, for their funeral rites are performed when they leave home and take to the open air. It would be a great mistake to suppose that such acts are in any way penitential; they much rather reflect a change of mind; the active life having been led in the imitation of the proceeding deity is now balanced by an imitation of the Deus absconditus.

The mere presence of these men in a society to which they no longer belong, by its affirmation of ultimate values, affects all values.[192] However many may be the pretenders and shirkers who may adopt this way of life for a variety of inadequate reasons, it still remains that if we think of the four castes as representing the essence of Hindu society, the super-social and anonymous life of the truly poor man, who voluntarily relinquishes all obligations and all rights, represents its quintessence. These are those that have denied themselves and left all, to "follow Me". The making of this highest election is open to all, regardless of social status. In this order of nobodies, no one will ask "Who, or what were you in the world?. The Hindu of any caste, or even a barbarian, can become a Nobody. Blessed is the man on whose tomb can be written, *Hic jacet nemo* (= here lies no-one).

These are already liberated from the chain of fate or necessity, to which only the psycho-physical vehicle remains attached until the end comes. Death in samadhi changes nothing essential.[193] Of their condition thereafter little more can be said than that they are. They are certainly not annihilated, for not only is the annihilation of anything real a metaphysical impossibility, but it is explicit that "Never have I not been, or hast thou not been, or ever shall not be".[194] We are told that the perfected self becomes a ray of the Sun, and a mover-at-will (kāmacārin CU.VII.25.2) up and down these worlds, assuming what shape and eating what food he will; just as in John, the saved "shall go in and out, and find pasture" (John 10.9).[195] These expressions are consistent with the doctrine of "distinction without difference" (*bhedābheda*) supposedly peculiar to Hindu "theism" but presupposed by the doctrine of the single essence and dual nature and by many Vedantic texts, including those of the *Brahmā Sutra*, not refuted by Śaṅkarācārya himself.[196] The doctrine itself

[192] "Blessed is the kingdom wherein dwells one of them; in an instant they will do more lasting good than all the outward actions ever done" (Meister Eckhart, Evans trans.I.102); and as he also says "while other people watch, they will be sleeping", cf. BG.II.69. For those whom *we* call "useless" are the "true pilots" (Plato, *Republic* 489f. and M.6.23—why Buddha was a hermit).

[193] Enneads IV.7.14 "Nothing from the realm of real being shall pass away".

[194] BG.II.12.

[195] RV.IX.113.9; JUB.III.28.3; SA.VII.22; BU.II.1.18; CU.VII.25.2, VIII.1.5-6; Mund.Up.III.1.4; Tait.Up.III.10.5; Pistis Sophia II.191b.

[196] *Brahmā Sutra* II.3.43f. Das Gupta, *Indian Philosophy*, II.42f. Also *Enneads* VI.6.7.

corresponds exactly to what is meant by Meister Eckhart's "fused but not confused".

How that can be we can best understand by the analogy of the relation of a ray of light to its source, which is also that of the radius of a circle to its centre. If we think of such a ray or radius as having "gone in" through the centre to an undimensioned and extra-cosmic infinity, nothing whatever can be said of it; if we think of it as at the centre, it is, but in identity with the centre and indistinguishable from it, and only when it goes "out" does it have an apparent position and identity. There is then a "descent" (*avataraṇa*)[197] of the Light of Lights as a light, but not as "another" light. Such a "descent" as that of Krishna or Rama differs essentially from the fatally determined incarnations of mortal natures that have forgotten Who they are; it is, indeed, their need that now determines the descent, and not any lack on his part who descends. Such a "descent" is of one "whose joy is only in himself",[198] and is not "seriously" involved in the forms he assumes, not by any coactive necessity, but only in "sport" (*krīḍā, līlā*).[199] Our immortal Self is "like the dewdrop on the lotus leaf",[200] tangent, but not adherent. "Ultimate, unheard, unreached, unthought, unbowed, unseen, undiscriminated and

[197] *Avataraṇa* = *Katābasis* as in *Republic* 519D and John III.13. The "return to the cave" of those who have made the "steep ascent" corresponds to the Sacrificer's re-descent for which references are given in note 166 (Hinduism).

Avatṛ varies in meaning from "come over" to "overcome", the latter meaning predominating in the earlier texts. The meaning "descend" is often expressed in other ways or by other verbs such as *avakram* or *avasthā, prati-i,* (*praty-*) *avaruh.* The earliest reference to Vishnu's "descent" may be TS.I.7.6.1, 2—*punar imaṁ lokam pratyavaroha.* Cf. ŚB.XI.2.3.3 where Brahma *imāṅ lokān . . . pratyavait.* In view of the later recognition that the Buddha was an *avatāra,* Cf. J.I.50 where the Buddha descends (*Oruyha* = *avaroha*) from the Tusita heaven to take birth, the illustration of this event at Bharhut inscribed *bhagavo okāmti* (=*avakrāmati*), and DhA.III.226 where he descends (otaritva = avatīrtva) from heaven at Saṅkassa. Cf. Windisch, *Buddha's Geburt,* 31f.

D.II.108 Buddha says: *yadā bodhisatto tusitā-kāyā cavitvā sato sampajāno* (cf. JUB) *mātu kucchim okkamati . . . matu kucchismā nikkhamati.*

For the idea of a "descent" otherwise phrased, see JUB.III.28.4; ŚB.I.9.3.10 and BG.IV.5f. Cf. *Clementine Homilies* III.20 "He alone has it (the spirit of Christ) who has changed his forms and his names from the beginning of the world and so reappeared again and again in the world".

[198] "*Che solo esso a sè piace*", Dante, *Purgatorio* XXVIII.91. Which Itself alone is pleasing to Itself.

[199] See note 76 and "Play and Seriousness" in *Journal of Philosophy* XXXIX.550-2. *Nitya* and *līlā,* the constant and the variable, are Being and Becoming, in Eternity and Time.—Enneads IV.8.5.

[200] CU.IV.14.3; MU.III.2; Sn.71, 213, 547 (like KU.V.11), 812, 845; A.II.39.

unspoken, albeit listener, thinker, seer, speaker, discriminator and fore-knower, of that Interior Person of all beings one should know that 'He is my Self'"[201] "That art thou"[202] (CU.VI.8.7).

[201]AA.III.2.4, Cf. AV.X.8.44; JUB.III.14.3; CU.IV.11.1, VI.8.7f; Kauṣ.Up.1:2, I.5.6, etc.

[202]SA.XIII; and the previous note. Other references on the theme: RV.X.7.6; ŚB.IX.2.3.27; Philo, *Fug.* 121-2, *Somn.*I.248; Diez.L.8.17,18(?)

> "All you have been, and seen, and done, and thought,
> Not you, but I, have seen and been and wrought . . .
> Pilgrim, Pilgrimage and Road
> Was but Myself toward Myself: and your
> Arrival but Myself at my own Door . . .
> Come, you lost Atoms, to your Centre draw . . .
> Rays that have wandered into Darkness wide,
> Return, and back into your Sun subside."
>
> Manṭiqu'ṭ—Ṭair (tr. Fitzgerald).

'I live, yet not I' *Gais.*II.20. "He exists formally and externally . . . but . . . is really non-existent as an individual agent and only 'persists' in virtue of the Divine life and energy which constitute his whole being."—Nicholson's Commentary on the *Mathnawī* I.128, III.3670.

BUDDHISM

INTRODUCTION

The more superficially one studies Buddhism, the more it seems to differ from the Brāhmaṇism in which it originated; the more profound our study, the more difficult it becomes to distinguish Buddhism from Brāhmaṇism, or to say in what respects, if any, Buddhism is really unorthodox. The outstanding distinction lies in the fact that Buddhist doctrine is propounded by an apparently historical founder, understood to have lived and taught in the sixth century B.C. Beyond this there are only broad distinctions of emphasis. It is taken almost for granted that one must have abandoned the world if the Way is to be followed and the doctrine understood. The teaching is addressed either to Brāhmaṇs who are forthwith converted, or to the congregation of monastic Wanderers (*pravrājaka*) who have already entered on the Path; others of whom are already perfected Arhats, and become in their turn the teachers of other disciples. There is an ethical teaching for laymen also, with injunctions and prohibitions as to what one should or should not do,[1] but nothing that can be described as a "social reform" or as a protest against the caste system. The repeated distinction of the "true Brāhmaṇ" from the mere Brāhmaṇ by birth is one that had already been drawn again and again in the Brāhmaṇical books.

If we can speak of the Buddha as a reformer at all it is only in the strictly etymological sense of the word: it is not to establish a new order but to restore an older form that the Buddha descended from heaven.[2] Although his teaching is "all just so and infallible",[3] this is because he has fully penetrated

[1]*Vinaya*, I.235 and passim; D.I.52, 68f.; S.III.208; A.I.62 (*Gradual Sayings*, p. 57, where Woodward's Footnote 2 is completely mistaken). The Buddha teaches that there is an ought-to-be-done (*kiriya*) and an ought-not-to-be-done (*akiriya*); these two words *never* refer to "the doctrine of Karma (retribution) and its opposite". Cf. HJAS.IV.1939, p.119. That the Goal (as in Brāhmaṇical doctrine) is one of liberation from good and evil both (see notes 105, 106 (Buddhism)) is quite another matter; the doing of good and avoidance of evil are indispensible to Wayfaring. The view that there is no-ought-to-be-done (*a-kiriya*), however argued, is heretical: responsibility cannot be evaded either (1) by the argument of a fatal determination by the causal efficacy of past acts or (2) by making God (*issaro*) responsible or (3) by a denial of causality and postulation of chance; ignorance is the root of all evil, and it is upon what we do now that our welfare depends (A.I.173f.). Man is helpless only to the extent that he sees Self in what is not-Self; to the extent that he frees himself from the notion "This is I", his actions will be good and not evil; while for so long as he identifies himself with soul-and-body (*saviññāna-kāya*) his actions will be "self"-ish.

[2]Confucius *Analects*—"A gentleman does not invent, but transmits".

Philo, Spec. IV.49—"No pronouncement of a prophet is ever his own".

[3]D.III.135 *tath'eva hoti no aññathā*; A.II.23; D.III.133; Sn.357 *yathā vādī tathā kārī*. (Cf. RV.IV.33.6 *satyam ūcur nara evā hi cakruḥ*); hence Sn.430, Itiv. 122, *tathāvādin*. In

the Eternal Law (*akālika dharma*)[4] and personally verified all things in heaven or earth;[5] he describes as a vile heresy the view that he is teaching a "philosophy of his own", thought out by himself.[6] No true philosopher ever came to destroy, but only to fulfil the Law. "I have seen", the Buddha says, "the ancient Way, the Old Road that was taken by the formerly All-Awakened, and that is the path I follow";[7] and since he elsewhere praises the Brāhmaṇs of old who remembered the Ancient Way that leads to Brahma,[8] there can be no doubt that the Buddha is alluding to "the ancient narrow path that stretches far away, whereby the contemplatives, knowers of Brahma, ascend, set free" (*vimuktāḥ*), mentioned in verses that were already old when Yājñavalkya cites them in the earliest Upanishad.[9]

---

this sense *ṭathāgato* can be applied to Buddha, Dhamma *and* Saṅgha, Sn.236-8 S.III.116f. cannot say *hoti, na hoti, hoti ca na hoti, neva hoti na na hoti.*

[4]The Dhamma taught by the Buddha, beautiful from first to last, is both of present application (*saṁdiṭṭhiko*) and timeless (*akāliko*), passim.

It follows that the same applies to the Buddha himself, who identifies himself with the Dhamma. Cf. *Epistle to Diognetus* V.2.

[5]D.I.150 *sayam abhiññā sacchikatvā*; D.III.135 *sabbam . . . abhisambuddham*; Dh.353 *sabbavidū'ham asmi.*

[6]*Epistle to Diognetus* V.3. (Apostolic Fathers, 359) M.I.68f., the Buddha "roars the Lion's roar" and having recounted his supernatural powers, continues: "Now if anyone says of me, Gotama the Pilgrim, knower and seer as aforesaid, that my eminent Aryan gnosis and insight have no superhuman quality, and that I teach a Law that has been beaten out by reasoning (*takka-pariyāhatam*) experimentally thought out and self-expressed (*sayam-patibhānam*), if he will not recant, not repent (*cittam pajahati = metanoein*) and abandon this view, he falls into hell". [D.I.16,22 Buddha's Knowledge is a priori (*pajānāti*), not inductive. D.I.45,79—to come to know truly]. "These profound truths (*ye dhamma gambhīrā*) which the Buddha teaches are inaccessible to reasoning (*atakkāvacarā*), he has verified them by his own super-knowledge" (D.I.22); cf. KU.II.9 "it is not by reasoning that that idea can be reached" (*naiṣā tarkeṇa matir āpaneyā*). Mil.217f. explains that it is an "ancient Way that had been lost that the Buddha opens up again". The reference is to the brahmacariya, "walking with God" (= *theo sunopa ein, Phaedrus* 248C; Philo *Migr.* 131, 126) of RV.X.109.5, AV., Brāhmaṇas, Upanisads and Pali texts, passim.

The "Lion's roar" is originally Bṛhaspati's, RV.X.67.9, i.e. Agni's. Also RV.I.65.5 "awakened at the dawn, he restores by his operations consciousness to men". And M.1.421—*asamayavimokham*, Eternal Deliverance.

Saint Thomas I.26.1. The will is free in so far as it obeys Reason, i.e. what one thinks is a blind and fettered will. Also *Nichomedian Ethics* IX.8.7.

[7]RV.X.130.7 *purveṣaṁ panthām anudṛśya.*

S.II.106 *purāṇam maggam purāṇañjasam . . . anugacchīm.*

Stobaei Hermetica IIB—". . . the road to truth which our ancestors travelled". See also Parmenides "Road of the Daimon"; *Philo*—"the roads of heaven are happy"; *Phaedrus* 247, Plato *Rep.* Bk.VII.

[8]S.IV.117; In *Ittivuttaka* 28,29 those who follow this (ancient) Way taught by the Buddhas are called Mahatmas. But, Sn. 284-315 says—"now that the Brāhmaṇs have long neglected their ancient Law, the Buddha preaches it again".

[9]BU.IV.4.8, RV.IV.18.1. As Mrs. Rhys Davids has also pointed out, the Buddha is a

On the other hand it is expressly stated that the Brāhmaṇs of today—although there are exceptions—have fallen from the graces that pertained to their pure and selfless ancestors.[10] It is from this point of view, and in connection with the fact that Buddha is born in an age when the royal caste is more than the priestly caste in honour, that we can best understand the reason of the promulgation of the Upanishads and Buddhism at one and the same time. These two closely related and concordant bodies of doctrine, both of "forest" origin, are not opposed to one another, but to a common enemy. The intention is clearly to restore the truths of an ancient doctrine. Not that the continuity of transmission in the lineages of the forest hermitages had ever been interrupted, but that the Brāhmaṇs at court and in the world, preoccupied with the outward forms of the ritual[11] and perhaps too much concerned for their emoluments, had now become rather "Brāhmaṇs by birth" (*brahmabandhu*) than Brāhmaṇs in the sense of the Upanishads and Buddhism, "knowers of Brahmā" (*brahmavit*).[12] There can be little doubt that the profound doctrine of the Self had hitherto been taught only in pupillary succession (*guruparamparā*) to qualified disciples; there is plenty of evidence for this on the one hand in the Upanishads themselves[13] (the word itself implies "sitting close to" a teacher) and on the other hand in the fact that the Buddha often speaks of "holding nothing back". The net result of these conditions would be that those to whom the Buddha so often refers as the "uninstructed multitude" must have entertained those mistaken "soul theories" and beliefs in the reincarnation of a "personality" against which the Buddha fulminates untiringly.[14]

It may well be, too, that kings themselves, opposing—their arrogant power

---

critic of Brāhmaṇism only in external matters; the "internal system of spiritual values" he "takes for granted" ("Relations between Early Buddhism and Brāhmaṇism", IHQ., X,1934, p. 282).

In view of the current impression that the Buddha came to destroy, not to fulfil an older Law, we have emphasized throughout the uninterrupted continuity of Brāhmaṇical and Buddhist doctrine (e.g. in note 159 (Buddhism)); Buddhist doctrine is original (*yoniso manasikaro*) indeed, but certainly not novel.

[10]Sn. 284f. (cf. RV.X.71.9); D.III.81, 82 and 94f.; exceptions, S.11.13; Sn.1082.

[11]See ŚB.IX.5.2.12,13 for the condemnation of professional sacrifices.

[12]So asserted Sn. 284f., that Brāhmaṇs nowadays do not follow *purānam brāhmaṇānan brahmanadhamma.*

[13]E.g. MU.VI.29 "This deepest mystery . . ."; BU.VI.3.12; BG.IV.3, XVIII.67. Yet the Upaniṣads were actually "published"; and just as the Buddha "holds nothing back", so we are told that "nothing whatever was omitted in what was told to Satyakāma, a man who cannot prove his ancestry, but is called a Brāhmaṇ because of his truth speaking (CU.IV.4.9). There is no more secrecy, and now whoever is a Comprehensor can properly be called a Brāhmaṇ (ŚB.XII.6.1.41).

[14]S.II.58 Buddha's knowledge of origin and end of *jarāmaranau* is identical with that of former and future *samanas* and *brahmans* and this is *anvaye ñānam,* the sequence of gnosis.

to sacerdotal control, had ceased to choose their Brāhmaṇ ministers wisely.[15] For that situation Indra himself, king of the Gods, "blinded by his own might" and misled by the Asuras, provides the archetype *in divinis.*[16] On the other hand, for the "awakening" of a royalty in the Buddha's case we have likewise in Indra the paradigm; for being admonished by the spiritual adviser to whom his allegiance is due, Indra "awakens himself" (*buddhvā cātmānam*),[17] and praises himself, the awakened Self,[18] in lauds in which we find the words, which the Buddha might have used, "Never at any time am I subject to Death" (*mṛtyu* = *māra*).[19] It will not be overlooked, too, that the Vedic Indra is more than once referred to as Arhat. And if it seems strange that the true doctrine should have been taught, in the Buddha's case, by a member of the royal caste, it is only the same situation that we sometimes meet with in the Upanishads themselves.[20] Was not Krishna also of royal blood, and yet a spiritual teacher? What all this amounts to is this, that when the salt of the "established church" has lost its savour, it is rather from without than from within that its life will be renewed.

The scriptures in which the traditions of the Buddha's life and teachings are preserved fall into two classes, those of the Narrow Way (Hinayāna) and those of the Broad Way (Mahāyāna). It is with the former, and on the whole older texts that we shall be chiefly concerned. The books pertaining to the "Narrow Way" are composed in Pali, a literary dialect closely related to Sanskrit. The Pali literature ranges in date from about the third century B.C. to the sixth century A.D. The Canon consists of what are called the "Three Baskets", respectively of monastic regimen (Vinaya), Discourse (Sūtra) and Abstract Doctrine (Abhidhamma). We shall be chiefly concerned with the five classes of the "Discourse" literature in which are preserved what are taken to be the Buddha's actual words. Of the extra-canonical literature the most important of the early books are the Milindapañha and the Visuddhimagga. The great Jātaka books, largely composed of ancient mythological materials recast in a popular form and retold as stories of the former births, is relatively late, but very instructive both for the Buddhist point of view and as a detailed picture of life in ancient India. All these books are provided with elaborate commentaries in what now would be called the "scholastic" manner. We shall take this literature as it stands; for we have no faith in the emendation of texts by modern scholars whose critical methods are mainly based on their dislike

[15]Cf. ŚB.IV.1.4.5.

[16]BD.VII.54.

[17]BD.VII.57.

[18]From the waking and sleeping dream of this world the word 'Buddha' is literally 'the Wake', and he is, in fact, like Agni 'awakened at dawn' (RV.I.65.5 *uṣarbudh*).

Refer BG.II.69 on 'sleep and waking' with S.I.107 and J.I.61.

[19]RV.X.48.5. The Buddha is *mārabhibhū*, Sn. 571, etc., as Indra is the conqueror of Vṛtra-Namuci; Cf. my "Some Sources of Buddhist Iconography", in *B.C. Law Volume* I, pp. 471-8, on the *Māra-dharṣana.*

[20]BU.VI.2.8; CU.V.3-11; Kaus.Up.IV.9 (where the situation is called 'abnormal", *pratiloma*).

of monastic institutions and their own view of what the Buddha ought to have said. It is in fact surprising that such a body of doctrine as the Buddhist, with its profoundly other-worldly and even anti-social emphasis, and in the Buddha's own words "hard to be understood by you who are of different views, another tolerance, other tastes, other allegiance and other training",[21] can have become even as "popular" as it is in the modern Western environment. We should have supposed that modern minds would have found in Brāhmaṇism, with its acceptance of life as a whole, a more congenial philosophy. We can only suppose that Buddhism has been so much admired mainly for what it is not. A well known modern writer on the subject has remarked that "Buddhism in its purity ignored the existence of a God; it denied the existence of a soul; it was not so much a religion as a code of ethics".[22] We can understand the appeal of this on the one hand to the

[21]D.III.40, cf. S.1.136, D.1.12, M.I.167.

[22]Winifred Stephens, *Legends of Indian Buddhism*, 1911, p. 7. Similarly M.V. Bhattacharya maintains that the Buddha taught that "there is no Self, or Ātman" (*Cultural Heritage of India*, p. 259). Even in 1925 a Buddhist scholar could write "The soul . . . is described in the Upanisads as a small creature in shape like a man . . . Buddhiṣm repudiated all such theories" (PTS Dictionary, s.v. attaṇ). It would be as reasonable to say that Christianity is materialistic because it speaks of an "inner man". Few scholars would write in this manner today, but ridiculous as such statements may appear, (and it is as much an ignorance of Christian doctrine as it is of Brāhmaṇism that is involved), they still survive in all popular accounts of "Buddhism".

Th. Scherbatsky—*Buddhist Logic* I.1932, p. 2.

Buddhism "denied a God, it denied the Soul, it denied Eternity"! Scherbatsky's *The Doctrine of the Buddha* (BSOS, VI.867f.) provides a good critique of Keith's demand to "lay aside our natural desire to find reason prevailing in a barbarous age", in his *Buddhist philosophy*, p. 29.

It is of course, true that the Buddha denied the existence of a "soul" or "self " in the narrow sense of the word (one might say, in accordance with the command, *deneget seipsum* (deny himself), Mark, VIII.34!) but this is not what our writers mean to say, or are understood by their readers to say; what they mean to say is that the Buddha denied the immortal, unborn and Supreme Self of the Upanishads. And that is palpably false. For he frequently speaks of this Self or Spirit, and nowhere more clearly than in the repeated formula *na me so attā*, "That is not my Self ", excluding body and the components of empirical consciousness, a statement to which the words of Śaṅkarā-cārya are peculiarly apposite, "Whenever we deny something unreal, it is with reference to something real" (*Neti, neti* in *Brahmā Sutra* III.2.22); as remarked by Mrs. Rhys Davids, "so, 'this one', is used in the Suttas for utmost emphasis in questions of personal identity" (*Minor Anthologies*, I, p. 7, note 2).

Na me so attā is no more a denial of the Self than Socrates' *to . . . sōma . . . ouk estin ho anthropos* = the body is not the man (*Aniochus* 365), is a denial of "the Man"! But Dh A IV.172 "*me sammāpaṇito attā*"! is positive. It was not for the Buddha, but for the natthika, to deny this Self! And so to "ignoring God" (it is often pretended that Buddhism is "atheistic"), one might as well argue that Meister Eckhart "ignored God" in saying "niht, daz ist gote gelich, wande beide niht sind" (God is not like God, for it is impossible for the two to be the same.)

rationalist and on the other to the sentimentalist. Unfortunately for these, all three statements are untrue, at least in the sense in which they are meant. It is with another Buddhism than this that we are in sympathy and are able to agree; and that is the Buddhism of the texts as they stand.

Of the texts of the Broad Way, composed in Sanskrit, few if any antedate the beginning of the Christian era. Amongst the most important of them are the Mahāvastu, the Lalita Vistara, the Divyāvadāna and the Saddharma Puṇḍarika. The two main forms of Buddhism to which we have referred are often spoken of, rather loosely, as respectively Southern and Northern. It is the Southern school that now survives in Ceylon, Burma and Siam. The two schools originally flourished together in Burma, Siam, Cambodia, Java and Bali, side by side with a Hinduism with which they often combined. Buddhism of the Northern school passed over into Tibet, China and Japan, through the work of Indian teachers and native disciples who made translations from Sanskrit. In those days it was not considered that the mere knowledge of languages sufficed to make a man a "translator" in any serious sense of the word; no one would have undertaken to translate a text who had not studied it for long years at the feet of a traditional and authoritative exponent of its teachings, and much less would any one have thought himself qualified to translate a book in the teachings of which he did not believe. Few indeed are the translations of Indian books into European languages that can yet come up to the standards set for themselves by the Tibetan and Chinese Buddhists.[23]

It may be observed that while Brāhmaṇism was at one time widely diffused in the "Greater India" of South East Asia, it never crossed the northern frontiers of India proper; Brāhmaṇism was not, like Buddhism, what might be called a missionary faith. Indian culture reached and profoundly influenced the Far East through Buddhism, which sometimes fused with and sometimes existed side by side with Taoism, Confucianism and Shinto. The greatest influence was exerted by the contemplative forms of Buddhism; what had been Dhyana in India became Cha'n in China and Zen in Japan.[24] We cannot, unfortunately, describe these forms of Buddhism here, but must affirm that although they often differ greatly in emphasis and detail from the Narrow Way, they represent anything but a degeneration of Buddhism; the Buddhisms of Tibet and the Far East are calculated to evoke our deepest sympathies, equally by their profundity of their doctrines and the poignant beauty of the literature and art in which these teachings are communicated. We have only to add that Buddhism had died out in India proper by the end of the twelfth century.

Śaṅkarācārya, the leading exponent of the Vedanta as a system, has often been called a Pracchannabauddha, "concealed Buddhist". The term Vedanta ("End of the Vedas" in the sense that the New Testament might be called the "conclusion and fulfilment" of the Old) occurs, however, already in the Upanishads; and the fact is that Vedanta and Buddhism have so much in

[23]See Marco Pallis, Peaks and Lamas, 1939, pp. 79-81; ed. 1974, pp. 72-4.

[24]See the various books of D.T. Suzuki.

common from the beginning that any exposition of either must sound like an exposition of the other. That is why a fusion of Hinduism and Buddhism takes place in the Indian Middle Ages and why Buddhism ceased to exist as a separate doctrine in India proper. If Buddhism rather than Hinduism could migrate to and survive elsewhere, this is mainly because while Hinduism fulfils itself in both the active and contemplative lives, Buddhism is chiefly concerned with the life of contemplation and can for that reason be the more easily taught as a Way of escape from the formal bonds of *any* social order.

THE MYTH

In asking, what is Buddhism, we must begin, as before, with the Myth. This has now become the Founder's life of some eighty years, into which period the whole epic of the victory over death has now been condensed. But if we subtract from the pseudo-historical narrative all its mythical and miraculous features, the residual nucleus of historically plausible fact will be very small indeed: and all that we can say is that while there may have lived an individual teacher who gave the ancient wisdom its pecularly "Buddhist" colouring, his personality is completely overshadowed, as he must have wished it should be,[25] by the eternal substance (*akālika dharma*) with which he identified himself. In other words, "the Buddha is only anthropomorphic, not a man".[26] It is true that a majority of modern scholars, euhemerist by temperament and training, suppose that this was not Man, but a man; subsequently deified; we take the contrary view, implied by the texts, that the Buddha is a solar deity descended from heaven to save both men and Gods from all the ill that is denoted by the word "mortality", the view that his birth and awakening are coeval with time.[27]

Before proceeding to the narrative we must explain how a distinction is made between the epithets Bodhisattva and Buddha. The Bodhisattva is an "awakening being", or one of "wakeful nature"; the Buddha is "awake" or "The Wake". The Bodhisattva is, dogmatically, an originally mortal being, qualifying by the making—become of transcendental virtues and insights for the "total awakening" of a Buddha. Gautama Siddhārtha, the "historical Buddha", is thus himself a Bodhisattva until the moment of his "all-awakening". It is, furthermore assumed that a Buddha is born in every successive aeon, and that Gautama Siddhārtha was the seventh in such a series of prophetic incarnations, and that he will be followed by Maitreya, now a Bodhisattva in heaven. There are other Bodhisattvas, notably Avalokiteśvara, who are

[25]Dh. 74 *mam'eva kata . . . iti bālassa saṅkappo*, "'I did it', an infantile idea", cf. note 6 (Buddhism).

[26]Kern, *Manual of Indian Buddhism*, p. 65. Cf. A.II.38,39 where the Buddha says that he has destroyed all the causes by which he might become a God or a man, etc., and being uncontaminated by the world, cf. Sn.558 (*abhiññeyam . . . tasmā buddho'smi* = "Therefore I am Buddha").

[27]*Saddharma Puṇḍarīka*, XV.1, in reply to the bewilderment of his audience, who cannot understand the Buddha's claim to have been the teacher of countless Bodhisattvas in bygone aeons. In just the same way Arjuna is bewildered by Krishna's eternal birth (BG.IV.4), and the Jews could not understand the saying of Christ, "before Abraham was, I am", i.e. "whose birth of Mary ghostly was more pleasing to him than his birth of Mary in the flesh"! Cf. Sim.IX.12.1 "The Son of God is older than all his creation" *Shephard of Hermas*. In Sim.V.6.5, 'The Holy Spirit' is identified with Christ, as *prāṇa* is equated to Agni.

virtually Buddhas, but are vowed never actually to enter into their Buddhahood until the last blade of grass has been first redeemed.

Previous to his last birth on earth, the Bodhisattva is resident in the Tuṣita heaven; and there being urged by the Gods to release the universe from its sorrows, he considers and decides upon the time and place of his birth and the family and mother of whom he will be born. A Buddha must be born of either a priestly or the royal caste, whichever is predominant at the time; and the royal caste being predominant then, he chooses to be born of Mahā Māyā, the queen of king Śuddhodana of the Śākya clan, at his capital city of Kapilavastu in the Middle Country; and that is to say, whatever else it may mean, in the "Middle Country" of the Ganges Valley. The Annunciation takes the form of "Mahā Māyā's dream", in which she sees a glorious white elephant descending from the skies to enter her womb. The king's interpreters of dreams explain that she has conceived a son who may be either a Universal Emperor or a Buddha. Both of these possibilities are actually realised in the spiritual sense, for while it is true that the Buddha's kingdom was not of this world, it is both as Teacher and as Lord of the universe that he "turns the wheel".

The child is visible in the mother's womb.[28] When the time comes, Mahā Māyā sets out to visit her parents at Devahrada; on her way she pauses at the Lumbini Park, and feeling that her time has come, she stretches out her hand to support herself by the branch of a tree, which bends down of its own accord. Standing thus, she gives painless birth to the child. The child is born from her side. It is not explicit, but can be presumed that the birth was "virgin"; in any case it is interesting that the story was already known to Hieronymus who mentions it in a discussion of Virginity and in connection with the miraculous births of Plato and Christ.[29] The child is received by the Guardian Deities of the Four Quarters. He steps down onto the ground, takes seven strides, and proclaims himself the "Foremost in the World". The whole universe is transfigured and rejoices in light. On the same day are born the "seven connatural ones", amongst whom are the Bodhisattva's future wife, his horse, and the disciple Ananda. These things take place, not uniquely, but "normally", that is to say that such is the course of events whenever a Buddha is born.

Mahā Māyā's dormition takes place a week after the child is born, and her

[28] Dom M. Britt, o.s.b., ed. *The Hymns of the Breviary and Missal*, N.Y. 1936:

Ventris obtuso recubans cubili,
Senseras Regem thalamo manentem
"Still resting in the concealed abode of the womb,
Thou (St. John) didst perceive thy King reposing in His chamber".

In its Christian context the motive is probably of Egyptian origin. Cf. H. Schaefer, *Von Aegyptischen Kunst*, 1930, Abb. 71, The New Sun visible in the womb of the Sky-goddess.

See also J.1.51; M. Windisch, *Buddha's Gerbart* 116f.

[29] *Libri adv. Jovinianum*, I.42.

sister Prajāpati, and co-wife of Suddhodana, takes her place. The child is taken back to Kapilavastu, and shown to the father; he is recognized and worshipped by the Brāhmaṇ soothsayers, who announce that he will be Emperor or Buddha, at the age of thirty five. The child is presented in the temple, where the tutelary deity of the Śākyas bows down to him. Śuddhodana, desiring that his son may be an Emperor and not a Buddha, and learning that he will abandon the world only after he has seen an old man, a sick man, a corpse and a monk, brings him up in luxurious seclusion, ignorant of the very existence of suffering and death. The first miracle takes place on a day when the king, in accordance with custom, is taking part in the First Ploughing of the year; the child is laid in the shadow of a tree, which does not move although the shadows of other trees move naturally with the sun; in other words, the sun remains overhead. The child at school learns with supernatural facility. At the age of sixteen, by victory in an archery contest, in which his arrow pierces seven trees, he obtains his cousin Yaśodhara as wife; she becomes the mother of a boy, Rahula.

In the meantime, on four successive days, while driving through the city to the pleasure park, the Bodhisattva has seen the four signs; for although all such signs have been banned from the city by royal edict, the Gods assume the forms of the old man, sick man, corpse and monk, and the Prince is made acquainted with age, illness, death and the serenity of a man who has risen above these vicissitudes of existence. He goes to his father and announces his intention of leaving the world and becoming a monk, in order to find out the way of escape from subjection to this mortality. The father cannot dissuade him, but keeps the palace gates closed. That night the Bodhisattva takes silent leave of his wife and child and calling for his horse, departs by the palace gate, miraculously opened for him by the Gods; he is accompanied only by his charioteer (*manas*).

Now Māra, Death, the Evil, offers him the empire of the whole world if he will return; failing in this temptation, he follows the Bodhisattva, to find another opportunity. Reaching the deep forests, the Bodhisattva cuts off his royal turban and long hair, unbecoming a pilgrim, and these are elevated by the God and enshrined in heaven. They provide him with a pilgrim's garment. He sends his charioteer back to the city with his horse; the latter dies of a broken heart.

The Bodhisattva now studies with Brāhmaṇ teachers and practises extreme mortifications. He finds five disciples, all of whom leave him when he abandons these ineffectual fastings. In the meantime Sujātā, the daughter of a farmer, who has been making offerings to the spirit of a banyan tree, now brings her gift of milkrice, into which the Gods have infused ambrosia; she finds the Bodhisattva seated beneath the tree, and gives him the rice in a golden bowl, and a golden ewer of water. She receives his blessings. He then goes down to the river to bathe, after which he eats the food, which is to last him for seven weeks. He casts the bowl into the river, and from the significant fact it floats upstream learns that he will succeed that very day. He returns to the Tree of the Awakening. At the same time Indra (the Dragon slayer, with

Agni, of our former lecture, and the type of the sacrificer in divinis) assumes the shape of a grass-cutter and offers to the Bodhisattva the eight bundles of grass that are used in sacrificial ritual. The Bodhisattva circumambulates the tree, and finally standing facing East finds that the circles of the world about him stand fast. He spreads the strew, and there rises up a throne or altar at the foot of the tree; he takes his seat thereon, determined never to rise again until he has attained the knowledge of the causation and cure of the evil of mortality. It is there at the navel of the earth, and at the foot of the Tree of Life, that all former Buddhas have awakened.[30]

Now Māra appears again and lays claim to the throne. The Bodhisattva touches the Earth, calling her to witness to the virtues by right of which he takes it; and she appears and gives witness. Māra, assisted by his demon army, now assaults the Bodhisattva with fire and darkness, and with showers of burning sand and ashes; but all his weapons fall harmlessly at the Bodhisattva's feet. At the first sight of Māra the Gods have fled, leaving the Bodhisattva all alone, but for the powers of the soul, his retainers; now Māra gives up the contest and the Gods return.

It is now nightfall. In the course of the night the Bodhisattva passes through all the stages of realisation until at dawn, having perfectly grasped the cycle of "Causal Origination" (*pratītya samutpāda*) he becomes wholly awakened, and is a Buddha. The whole universe is transfigured and rejoices. The Buddha breaks into his famous song of victory:

Seeking the builder of the house
I have run my course in the vortex
Of countless births, never escaping the hobble (of death);
Ill is repeated birth after birth!
Householder, art seen!
Never again shalt thou build me a house
All of thy rigging is broken,
The peak of the roof is shattered:[31]
Its aggregations passed away,
Mind has reached the destruction of cravings.

The Buddha remains for seven weeks within the circle of the Tree of the Awakening, enjoying the gladness of release. Of the events of these weeks two are significant, first the temptation by the daughters of Māra, who attempt to win by their charms what their father could not gain by his power: and secondly the hesitation to teach; the Buddha hesitates to put in motion the Wheel of the Law, thinking that it will not be understood and that this will be

[30]D.II.85 Buddha preaching to Brethren.
Majjhimam thambam Nissaya pur atthabhi mukho nisidi.

[31]This is a technicality. See my "Symbolism of the Dome" (Part 3) in IHQ.XIV, 1938 and "Svayamātṛṇṇā; Janua Coeli" in *Zalmoxis* II, 1939 (1941).

Shams-i-Tabrīz XXXIV.3 "Or is it Thou who makest a ruin of every house I build?"

the occasion of needless anguish to himself; the Gods exclaim at this, "The world is lost", and led by Brahmā persuade the Buddha that some are ripe for understanding. The Buddha, accordingly, sets out for Benares and there in the "First Preaching" sets the Wheel of the Law in motion, and in the second preaches that there is no individual constant underlying the forms of our consciousness. In other words, in the doctrine of the un-self-ish-ness (*anātmya*) of all physical and mental operations he dismisses the popular *Cogito ergo sum* as a crude delusion and the root of all evil. By these sermons he converts the five disciples who had formerly deserted him; and there are now five Arhats, that is to say five "despirated" (*nirvāta*) beings in the world.

From Benares the Buddha went on to Uruvelā, near the modern Bodhgayā, and finds on the way a party of thirty young men picnicking, with their wives. One of them had no wife, and had brought a woman with him, who had just stolen their belongings and run away. All the young men ask the Buddha whether he has seen such a woman. The Buddha replies, "What now, young men, do you think? Which were the better for you, to go tracking the woman, or to go tracking the Self?" (*ātmānam gavis*).[32] They reply that it were better to seek the Self, and are converted. Here for the first time we meet with the Buddha's doctrine of a real Self. At Uruvelā he reaches the hermitage of a community of Brāhmaṇical Fire-worshippers, and wishes to spend the night in their fire temple. They warn him that it is the haunt of a fierce Dragon that may hurt him. The Buddha thinks not, and retires for the night, seating himself cross-legged and vigilant. The Dragon is infuriated. The Buddha will not destroy it, but will overcome it; assuming his own fiery form, and becoming a "human Dragon", he fights fire with fire, and in the morning appears with the tamed Dragon in his alms-bowl.[33] Upon another day the fire-worshippers are unable to split their wood, or light or extinguish their fires until the Buddha permits it. In the end the Brāhmaṇs abandon their Burnt-offerings (*agnihotra*) and become disciples of the Buddha. In this connection we must cite the instance of another Brāhmaṇ fire-worshipper, to whom in the course of their dialogue the Buddha says,

> I pile no wood for fires or altars;
> I kindle a flame within me,—
> My heart the hearth, the flame the dompted self.[34]

[32]Vin.I.23 (Mahavagga I.14). Cf. Vis.393 *rājānaṁ gavesitum udāhu attānam?* CU.VIII.7.1 *ya ātmā . . . sônveṣtavyaḥ.*

Visuddhi Magga 393—mumbling. Buddha makes King Mahā Kappina mumble. Queen Anoga says "Perhaps Lord, you have seen the king?" He said "Which is better, to seek the king or to seek the Self?"

(*Kim pana vo rājānaṁ gavesitum varam udahu attānaṁ ti*). Queen answers *attānamti*; accordingly he *dhammam deseti.* Cf. Also *Mahāvagga* I.23.

[33]Vin.I.25 (Mahāvagga I.15). Cf. the similar story of Mogallana's conflict with the Dragon Rāṣṭrapāla, Vis. 399f.

[34]S.I.169. See also my "Ātmayajña: Self-Sacrifice" in HJAS.VI.1942; rpt. in Coomaraswamy 2: *Selected Papers*, 1977.

We perceive that the Buddha is here simply carrying on the teaching of the Brāhmaṇical *Āraṇyaka* in which, as remarked by Keith, "the internal Agnihotra is minutely described as a substitute for the formal sacrifice".[35]

Time will not permit us to relate in detail the later events of the Buddha's life. He gradually builds up a large following of monastic wanderers like himself; somewhat against his will women were also allowed to be ordained as nuns; and by the end of his life there had developed an organised body of monks and nuns, many of whom lived in monasteries or nunneries, which had been donated to the community by pious laymen. The Buddha's life was spent in the care of the monastic community, and in preaching, either to assemblies of monks or to audiences of Brāhmaṇs, in disputations with whom he is invariably successful; he also performs many miracles. At last he announces his imminent death. When Ananda protests, he reminds him that while there will be those who are still addicted to mundane ways of thinking and will weep and roll in anguish, crying out—"Too soon will the Eye in the World pass away", there will be others, calm and self-possessed, who will reflect that all component things are impermanent, and that whatever has been born contains within itself the inherent necessity of dissolution: "Those will honour my memory truly, who live in accordance with the Way I have taught". When a believer comes to visit him, before he dies, the Buddha says, "What good will it do you to see this unclean body? He who sees the *Law* sees me, he who sees *me*, sees the Law (*dharma*)".[36] In announcing his forthcoming decease, the Buddha leaves this message, "Be such as have the Self (*ātman*) as your lamp, Self as only refuge, the Law as lamp and only refuge".[37]

[35]Cf. Keith, *Śāṅkhayana Āraṇyaka,* 1908, p. xi.

One must assume that it is in ignorance of the Brāhmaṇical literature that Mrs. Rhys Davids finds something novel in the Buddha's Internal Agnihotra (*Gotama the Man*, p. 97). Cf. My *Ātmayajña* . . . (1977), p. 129; and Good enough E.R.—*An Introduction to Philo Judaeus*, 1940, p.112, on old and new sacrifices. In just the same way I.B. Horner (*Early Buddhist Theory of Man Perfected,* Ch. II, esp. p. 53) can discuss the history of word arahat at great length without mentioning that in RV.X.63.4 we are told that the Gods (who, in their pluarality, had never been thought of as originally immortal) "by their worth (*arhaṇā*) attained their immortality"! And in the same way the PTS Pali Dictionary knows of *arahant* "before Buddhism" only as an "honorific title of high officials". Buddhist exegesis by scholars who do not know their Vedas is never quite reliable.

[36]S.III.120.

[37]D.II.101 *atta-dīpā viharatha atta-saraṇā . . . dhamma-dīpā dhamma saraṇā.* Cf. Sn. 501 *ye atta-dīpā vicaranti loke akiṁcanā sabbadhi vippamutta*; Dh.146, 232 *andhakārena onaddhā padīpaṁ na gavess atha . . . so karohi dīpam attano* (*dīpa* = island). The admonition "Make the Self your refuge" (*kareyya saraṇattano,* S.III.143) enjoins what the Buddha himself has done, who says "I have made the Self my refuge" (*katam me saraṇam attano,* D.II.120); for, indeed, "as he teaches, so he does" (*yathā vādi, tathā kāri,* A.II.23, III.135, Sn. 357); which *tathā* is often made the basis of the epithet "Tathāgata".

The Buddhist "lamp" texts correspond to Svet.Up.II.15 "When the bridled man by means of his own Self-suchness, as if by the light of a lamp (*ātma-tatvena* . . .

He explains that what this means in practice is a life of incessant recollectedness (*smṛti*). The Buddhist emphasis on mindfulness can hardly be exaggerated; nothing is to be done absentmindedly; or with respect to which one could say "I did not mean to do it"; an inadvertent sin is worse than a deliberate sin.[38] That means, that one must not simply "behave", instinctively; or as Plato expresses it, "Do nothing but in accordance with the leading of the immanent Principle, nothing against the common Law that rules the whole body, never yielding to the pulls of the affections, whether for good or evil; and this is what 'Self-mastery' means".[39] At the same time it must not be overlooked that behind this ethical application of mindfulness to conduct there lies a metaphysical doctrine; for Buddhism, like the Upanishads, regards all recognition not as an acquisition of new facts but as the recovery of a latent and ultimately unlimited omniscience; as in the Platonic doctrine, where all teaching and experience are to be thought of simply as reminders of what was already known but had been forgotten.[40]

Plato, again, continually reminds us that there are two in us, and that of these two souls or selves the immortal is our "real Self". This distinction of an immortal spirit from the mortal soul, which we have already recognized in Brāhmaṇism, is in fact the fundamental doctrine of the Philosophia Perennis wherever we find it. The spirit returns to God who gave it when the dust returns to the dust. *Gnōthi seauton* (= Know thyself); *Si ignoras te, egredere* (= If you are ignorant of yourself, begone). "Whither I go, *ye* cannot follow me now . . . If any man would follow me, let him deny himself ".[41] We must not

dīpopāmena), perceives the Brahma-suchness, unborn, steadfast, clean of all other suchness, then knowing God he is liberated from all ills". The Spirit (ātman) is our light when all other lights have gone out (BU.IV.3.6).

[38]On *sati* (*smṛti*) as "watching one's step", "discretion", cf. I. Cor.10.31, Cf.D.I.70, ŚBB.III.233, etc. Thus an inadvertent sin is worse than a deliberate sin (Mil.84, cf.158).

But like the Brāhmaṇical *smṛti* (*smara* also has the meaning "love"), the Buddhist *sati* means more than this mere heedfulness, the *padasaññam* of J.VI.252. Recollection is practised with a view to omniscience or super-gnosis (*abhiñña, pajānanā, prometheia, pronoia* = forethought, foresight, etc.) The fullest account is given in Vis.407f. In Mil.77-9, this is a matter either of intuitive, spontaneous and unaided super-gnosis, or occasioned (*kaṭumika* = *kṛtrima*); in the latter case we are merely reminded by external signs of what we already know potentially. Comparing this with Pras.Up.IV.5; CU.VII.13, VII.26.1 and MU.VI.7 ("The Self knows everything"), and taking account of the epithet Jātavedas = Pali *jātissaro,* it appears that the Indian doctrine of Memory coincides with the Platonic doctrine in Meno 81 (*mathēsis* = *anamnēsis,* i.e. learning = recollection).

[39]*Laws* 644, 645.

[40]Plato—*Meno.* 81,82; *Republic* 431A,B,604B; *Laws* 959B; *Phaedo* 83B, etc. See also my "*Recollection, Indian and Platonic*", JAOS. Supplement No.3, 1944 and *Coomaraswamy 2: Selected Papers,* Prin. Univ. Press, 1977, pp. 49-65.

[41]John XIII.36; Mark VIII.34. Those who do follow him have "forsaken all", and this naturally includes "themselves".

delude ourselves by supposing that the words *denegat seipsum* (= let him deny himself) are to be taken ethically (which would be to substitute means for ends); what they mean is understood by St. Bernard when he says that one ought *deficere a se tota, a semetipsa liques cere* (= one must totally abandon oneself, like a candle that burns itself up.) and by Meister Eckhart when he says that "The kingdom of God is for none but the thoroughly dead". "The word of God extends to the sundering of soul from spirit";[42] and it might well have been said by the Wake that "No man can be my disciple but and if he hate his own soul" (*kai ou misei—tēn heautou psuchēn* = he who does not hate—his own soul).[43] "The soul must put itself to death"—"Lest the Last Judgment come and find me unannihilate, and I be siez'd and giv'n into the hands of my own selfhood".[44]

[42]Epistle of Paul to the Hebrews (N.T.), IV.12.

[43]Luke XIV.26, "Who hateth not father and mother, and wife and children, and brethren and sisters", cf. MU.VI.28 "If to wife and family he be attached, for such a man, no, never at all", and Sn. 60 "Alone I fare, forsaking wife and child, mother and father". Cf. note 118 in 'Hinduism' section.

[44]Meister Eckhart and William Blake. Cf. Behmen, *Sex Puncta Theosophica*, VII.10 "Thus we see how a life perishes . . . namely, when it will be its own lord . . . If it will not give itself up to death, then it cannot obtain any other world". Cf. Matth.XV.25; *Phaedo*, 67, 68. "No creature can attain a higher grade of nature without ceasing to exist" (St. Thomas Aquinas, *Sum.Theol.* I.63.3). Cf. Schiller, "In error only there is life and knowledge must be death"; and what has been said above on Nirvana as a being *finished.* What lies beyond such deaths cannot be defined in terms of our kind of living. · Dante—*The Divine Comedy, Paradise* XIV.25.

Whoso laments, that we must doff this garb
of frail mortality, thenceforth to live
Immortally above; he hath not seen
The sweet refreshing of that heavenly shower.

THE DOCTRINE

In the Buddha's question cited above, "Were it not better if ye sought the Self?" the contrast of the plural verb with its singular object is precise. It is One that the many are to find. Let us consider some of the many other Buddhist contexts in which our selves, respectively composite and mortal and single and immortal, are contrasted. The question is asked, just as it had been in the Brāhmaṇical books, "By which self (*kena ātmanā*)[45] does one attain the Brahma-world?" The answer is given in another passage, where the usual formula descriptive of the Arhat's attainment concludes "with the Self that is Brahma—become" (*brahma-bhūtena ātmanā*); just as in the Upanishad "It is as Brahma that he returns to Brahma".[46] From that world there is no returning (*punarāvartana*) by any necessity of rebirth.[47] Other passages distinguish the Great Self (*mahātman*) from the little self (*alpātman*) or Fair Self (*kalyāṇātman*)

[45]Sn. 508 *Ko sujjhati muccati bajjhati ca? ken'attanā gacchati brahmalokam?* The obvious answers implied are Yakkha as in Sn. 875 and *brahma-bhūtena attanā* as in A.II.211: the Brāhmaṇical answers, AA.II.6 *prajñānam brahma; sa etena prajñenātmanā... —amṛtaḥ samabhavat*, BU.IV.4.6 *brahmaiva san brahmāpyeti* (with Śaṅkaracārya's comment that it is only of the Paramātmā that bondage and liberation can be predicated) are essentially the same; as in BG.XVIII.54 *brahma-bhūtah prasannātmā*. Sn. continues Bhagava hi me sakhi brahm 'ajja diṭṭho. 'I' = not Self; Self = not 'I'. Dh 62 perhaps "there is no self of Self" meaning is as Sonsare not "mine" so Self has no "my self".

It is characteristic of Lord Chalmer's attenuations that he renders *ken'attanā* only as "Whereby?". In the same way the PTS Dictionary carefully omits the positive references s.v. *attā* and ignores *mahattā*. Mrs. Rhys Davids has discussed *mahattā* = *mahātma* (e.g. *Review of Religion* VI.22f.), but ignores the nature of the *mahimaṇ* (majesty) on which the epithet depends.

[46]A.II.211 *brahma-bhūtena attanā viharati*; like BU.IV.4.6 *brahmaiva san brahmāpyeti*, and BG.XVIII.54 *brahmabhūtaḥ* BG.V.24 *brahma-nirvāṇa*. Cf. Sn. 508 *bhagavā hi me sakkhi brahma'jja diṭṭho; sakkhi* as in BU.III.4.2 *sākṣād-aparokṣādbrahma*. No Indian auditor in centuries B.C. could have supposed that a reference to Brahmā was meant. Cf. Sn. 479 *brahmā hi sakkhi*, 934 *sakkhi dhamma*; A.I.149 *sakkhi attā*; Muṇd Up. III.2.9 *sa yo ha brahmaveda . . . brahmana bhavati*; AA.II.6 *prajñenātmanā*; S.I.197 *brahmabhūta* in connection with arahat formula.

[I.B. Horner in a letter to AKC d. 18-11-'45: "As to Sn. 508 one translator (Chalmers) must have got Brahmā from the PTS edition of the Commentary. If you see *Woven Cadences*, as I hope you will, you will find the translator (E.M. Hare) has Brahm". Horner continues in her letter of 26-11-'45 : "I certainly agree with you about Dial.III.78. Surely such terms as *-ja, -nimitta, -dāyāda*, also *-bhūta*, in connection with brahma mean Brahmā *Brahmā-bhūtena attana viharati* at A.II.206 must mean Brahma—become".

[47]DA.I.313 *tato brahma-lokā paṭisandhi-vasena na āvattanadhammo*, expanding D.I.156 *anāvattidhammo*; as in BU.VI.2.15 te *teṣu brahmalokeṣu . . . vasanti, teṣāṁ na punarāvṛttiḥ*; CU.IV.15.5 *imam manāvamavartaṁ nāvartante*, CU.VIII.15.1 *Brahmasākṣātkar*.

There is, however, a distinction of salvation from perfection; to have become a

from foul (*pāpātman*);[48] the former is the latter's judge.[49] "The Self is the Lord of the self, and its goal."[50] In the saying "For one who has attained, there is not dearer than Self "[51] we recognize the doctrine of the Upanishads that the "Self alone is truly dear"[52] the Hermetic "Love thy Self ",[53] and the Christian doctrine that "A man, out of charity, ought to love himself more than he loves any other person",[54] i.e. that Self for whose sake he must deny himself.[55]

Brahmā in the Brahmā-world is a great achievement, but not the last step, a final exit (*uttarakaraṇīyam, uttarim nissaraṇam*), a de-spiration free from all factors of existence in time (*anupādisesa-nibbānam*) attainable by a Brahmā even in the Brahmā-world. The only condition superior to this is the attainment of this last end here and now (*jīvanmukti*), rather than post mortem (M.II.195-6, D.I.156, A.IV.76-7; cf. BU.IV.3.33 where Janaka, informed about the beatific Brahmā-world, demands "more than that, for my liberation").

These texts make it evident that in the common equation *brahmobhūto = buddho*, it is not "Brahmā-become", but "Brahma-become" that must be understood: the Bodhisatta had been already a Brahmā, and Mahā Brahmā, in former lives (A.IV.88), but for all that was not yet a Buddha, cf. MU.VI.22 where it is a question of transcending the audible Brahma and of "going home" to the supreme, inaudible Brahma in whom (or which) all individual characteristics (*pṛthag-dharminaḥ*) are merged, as in Sn. 1074-6 where the Muni, freed from name and aspect, "goes home", and of such there is nothing that can be said because all individual characteristics have been confused (*sabbesu dhammesu samūhatesu*), i.e. as when rivers reach the sea, A.IV.198.

[48]For references on *mahat, alpa*, see: BG.XVI.9 *naṣṭātmāno alpabuddhayaḥ*, XVIII.22 *atattvārthavadalpaṁ*; CU.VII.23.1 *nālpe sukhamasti*, VII.24.1 *yatra . . . -anyadvijānāti tadalpaṁ . . . tanmartyam*; KU.I.26 *sarvaṁ jīvitamalpameva*; also in Plato, *Republic* 519 the petty soul, *to psucharōn*, *Republic* 524 C intelligible and visible.

[49]A.I.57, 58, 87 (*attā pi attānam upavadati*), 149, 249; A.V.88; Sn. 778, 913, Cf. Manu XI.230; *Republic* 440 B; I Cor. 4.4. This is the "Ayenbyte of Inwyt", the Celtic "land of no return".

[50]Dh. 160 *attā hi attano nātho*; 380 *attā hi attano gati* (cf. BU.IV.3.32; KU.III.11; MU.VI.7 *ātmano'tmā netā amṛtākhyaḥ*; RV.V.50.1 *viśvo devasya neṭuḥ*, viz. Savitṛ). But in Dh. 62 *attā hi attano n'atthi*; "In self there's naught of Self"; S.IV.250 *sāram . . . -attano.* Cf. S.III.82,83 *yad anattā . . . na me so attā*, "What is not-Self, that's not my Self ", the referents are reversed; the Self (*ātman*) is selfless (*anātmya*) as in TU.II.7.

'I' = not-Self; Self = not-'I'. Dh.62 perhaps "there is no Self of self "!; but meaning is—as sons are not "mine", so Self has no "my"self.

[51]S.I.75 *n'ev'ajjhagā piyataram attanā kvaci . . . -attakāmo; udāna* 47; A.12.91 (cf.II.21) *attakāmena mahattam abhikkhaṅkatā* S.I.71,72, like BG.VI.5-7, explains when the Self is dear (*piyo*) and not dear (*appiyo*) to self. On the other hand in A.IV.97 *attā hi paramo piyo*, the man "too fond of himself " is what is ordinarily meant by the "selfish" man.

[52]BU.I.4.8, II.4, IV.5.

[53]Hermes, *Lib.* IV.6 B.

[54]St. Thomas Aquinas, *Sum. Theol.* II-II.26.4; cf. Dh.166 (man's first duty to work out his own salvation). A.V.90 and passim, *brahma-cariya* is rendered "Brahmā-life" (F.L. Woodward in his translation of *Anguttara Nikāya*).

[55]Cf. Plato, *Laws* 903D, "Soul, being conjoined now with one body, now with

In the Brāhmaṇical doctrine, our immortal, impassible, beatific inner Self and Person, one and the same in all beings, is the immanent Brahma, God within you.[56] He does not come from anywhere nor become anyone.[57] "That" is; but nothing else that is true can be said of it: "Thou canst not know the maker-to-know what is known, who is your Self in all things".[58] Just as God himself does not know *what* he is, because he is not any what.[59] The Buddhist doctrine proceeds in the same way, by elimination. Our own constitution and that of the world is repeatedly analysed, and as each one of the five physical and mental factors of the transient personality with which the "untaught many folk" identify "themselves" is listed, the pronouncement follows, "*That* is not myself " (*na me so ātmā*).[60] You will observe that amongst these childish mentalities who identify themselves with their accidents, the Buddha would have included Descartes, with his *Cogito ergo sum.*[61]

There is, in fact, no more an individual than there is a world soul. What we call our "consciousness" is nothing but a process; its content changes from day to day and is just as much causally determined as is the content of the body.[62] Our personality is constantly being destroyed and

---

another undergoes all sorts of changes . . . ". Augustine, *Sermons* CCXLI.3.3—on 'the mutability of soul *and* body', and—'belief in soul more dangerous than belief in body'.

[56]RV.I.115.1 *ātmā jagatastasthuṣaśca*; ŚB.X.4.2.27 *sarvessām bhūtānām ātmā*; BU.II.5.15 *sarvessām bhutānāmadhipatiḥ*; BU.III.5.1 *brahma, ya ātmā sarvāntaraḥ*; MU.V.1 *viśvātmā*; BG.VI.29 *sarvabhūtastham ātmānam*, BG.VII.9 *jīvanaṁ sarvabhūteṣu*; Manu I.54 *sarvabhūtātmā*, etc. This doctrine of one "Soul" or "Self " behind what appear to be our many different souls or selves can be recognized in Plato (notably *Meno* 81, describing the universal birth and consequent omniscience of the "Immortal Soul", cf. note 38 (Buddhism)), Plotinus (notably *Enneads* IV.9 passim, on the "reduction of all souls to one") and Hermes (notably *Lib.*V.10.A "bodiless and having many bodies, or rather present in all bodies", cf. KU.II.22 *aśarīram śarīreṣu*; KU.V.12 *sarvabhūtantarātmā*, "the essence of all beings"). It survives in Dionysius. "Being that pervades all things at once though not affected by them" (*De div.nom.*II.10).

[57]KU.II.18 *nāyam kutaścin na babhūva kaścit*; KU.II.25 *ka itthā veda yatra saḥ?* KU.VI.13 *asti iti eva* . . . . Cf. Mil.73 *bhagavā atthi* . . . *-na sakkā* . . . *nidassetuṁ idha va idha*; and Śaṅkaracārya (on BU.III.3) *muktasya ca na gatiḥ kvacit.*

[58]BU.III.4.2; Cf.II.4.14, IV.5.15; AA.III.2.4.

[59]Erivgena.

[60]A.II.177 "I am naught of an anyone anywhere, nor is there anywhere aught of mine"; similarly M.II.263, 264; Sn. 950, 951; Plotinus, *Enneads* VI.9.10 "But this man has now become another, and is neither himself nor his own". Cf. my "Ākimcaññā: Self Naughting" in *New Indian Antiquary*, 1940 and in 2 : *Selected Papers*, 1977, pp. 88-106. Also in *The Cloud of Unknowing*, Ch. 68 "Let be this everywhere and this aught, in comparison of this nowhere and this naught".

[61]If in S.III.105 where *upādāya asmīti* is equated to cogito ergo sum, but *rūpam, vedanam, saññānam, sankhāre* and *viññānam* are *anicca*, how then '*asmi*'?

[62]S.II.13, III.165, etc., *anniccau dukkhau anattā*, S.III.41, etc., like BU.III.4.2 *atônyadārtam.*

As St. Augustine says (*Sermo* CCXLI.2.2), body and soul alike are mutable, and those who recognized that this is so went in search of That which is unchanging.

renewed;[63] there is neither self nor anything of the nature of self in the world; and all this applies to all beings, or rather becomings, whether of men or Gods, now and hereafter. Just as it is expressed by Plutarch, "Nobody remains one person, nor is one person . . . Our senses, through ignorance of reality, falsely tell us that what appears to be, actually is".[64] The old Brāhmaṇical (and Platonic) symbol of the chariot is made use of; the chariot, with all its appurtenances, corresponds to what we call our self; there was no chariot before its parts were put together, and will be none when they fall to pieces; there is no "chariot" apart from its parts; "chariot" is nothing but a name, given for convenience to a certain continuum of perceptions, but must not be taken to be an entity (*sattva*); and in the same way with ourselves who are, just like the chariot, "confections". The Comprehensor has seen things "as they have become" (*yathā bhūtam*), causally arising and disappearing, and has distinguished himself from all of them; it is not for him, but only for an ignoramus to ask such questions as "Am I?", "What was I once?", "Whence did I come?", "Whither am I going?"[65] If the Arhat is expressly permitted still to say "I", this is only for convenience; he has long since outgrown all belief in a personality of his own.[66] But none of all this means, nor is it anywhere said that "There is no Self ".[67] On the contrary, there are passages in which when the five constituents of our evanescent and unreal "existence" have been listed, we find, not the usual formula of negation, "That is not my Self ", but the positive injunction, "Take refuge in the Self ";[68] just the Buddha also says that he himself has done.[69]

The empirical personality of this man, So-and-so, being merely a process, it is not "my" consciousness or personality that can survive death and be born again.[70] It is improper to ask "Whose consciousness is this?"; we should ask

[63]S.II.95, *viññānam . . . rattiyā ca divassassa ca ānnad eva upajjati aññaṁ nirujjhati.* See also note 70 (Buddhism) *Alaya vijñāna,* Cf. *Enneads* IV.7.12, VI.6.7, and Epicharmos Gr. 2 (Diels) in John Burnet, *Early Greek Philosophy,* 1920, p.152, note 1.

[64]Plutarch, *Moralia* 392D, based on Plato, *Symposium* 207D, E and *Phaedo* 78C. Burnet, p.152, cites the *First* step in wisdom by method and mortification.

Euthydemus 284D equates change with death, and Eckhart likewise equates death and change.

Cf. The "life of experience which is momentarily reborn in every fleeting instant", and Bowman's "specious present" in *Studies in the Philosophy of Religion* 2.346.

In this life we are the *subject* of experience; not the *substance* that *understands* it.

[65]S.II.26, 27. The enlightened disciple does not think of *himself* as transmigrating, but only recognizes the incessant operation of mediate causes in accordance with which contingent personalities arise and cease.

[66]S.I.14, D.I.202. Buddhism uses *attā-paḷitabho* terms conveniently but *apāramasau.*

[67]S.II.94. Better to think of *kāya* than of soul as 'self': both mutable. Cf. Augustine *Sermo.* CCXLI 3.3 (*Synthesis,* p.116).

[68]S.III.143. See note 37 (Buddhism).

[69]D.II.120. See note 37 (Buddhism).

[70]M.I.256 (Sati's heresy).

only, "How did this consciousness arise".[71] The old answer is given,[72] "The body is not 'mine', but an effect of past works".[73] There is no "essence" that passes over from one habitation to another; as one flame is lit from another, so life is transmitted, but not a life, not "my" life.[74] Beings are the heirs of acts;[75] but it cannot be said exactly that "I" now reap the rewards of what "I" did in a former habitation. There is causal continuity, but no one consciousness (*vijñāna*), no essence (*sattva*) that now experiences the fruits of good and evil actions, and that also recurs and reincarnates (*sandhāvati saṁsarati*) without otherness (*ananyam*)", to experience in the future the consequences of what is now taking place.[76] Consciousness, indeed is never the same from one day to another.[77] How, then, could "it" survive and pass over from one life to

[71]S.II.13, II.61, etc.

[72]AA.II.1.3 "Man is a product of works", i.e. of things that have been done up to that moment at which we speak (*karma-kṛtam ayam puruṣah*). Cf. BU.III.2.13 "... it is Karma alone that remains to reincarnate". See also notes 101 (Hinduism), and 64, 142 (Buddhism).

Cf. A.III.70 and A.V.88 for *kammadāyādo*, etc. As per M.I.483 householders are not saved but go to heaven; the ajivika is saved by belief in *karma.*

J. Grenier *La Choise* (Nowelle Encyclopedie Philosophique, p. 116).

Karma: "Chaque etre n'agit que selon sa propre nature,

mais il faccoune cette nature par chacun de ces actes" "each person only acts in accord with his own nature but he modifies this nature with each of his acts."

[73]S.II.64; S.I.38 *Satto saṁsāram āpādi, kammam asya parāyanam.* Cf. Chuang Tzu— "Change and decay in all around I see; O Thou who changest not, abide with Me".

[74]Mil. 71/2. That nothing but the "fire" of life is transmitted is in perfect agreement with the Vedantic "The Lord is the only transmigrant" and with Heracleitus, for whom the flux is only of the fontal and inflowing fire, *pur aeizdoon* (everliving fire) = Agni, *viśvāyus.* Not therefore in disagreement with Plato *et al.*, who certainly did not reject the "flux", but presumes a Being from which all becoming proceeds, a Being that is not itself a "thing", but from which all "things" incessantly flow.

M.I.115 *yañ-ñadeva bhikhave bhikhhu bahulum anivitakketi anuvicareti tathā tathā nati hoti cetaso.*

[75]M.I.390; S.II.64; A.V.88 "My nature is of works (*kammassako'mhi*), works I inherit, I am born of works, the kinsman of works, one to whom works revert; whatever work, or fair or foul, I do, I shall inherit". The last must not, of course, be taken to mean that an "I" really incarnates, but only that a future "I" will inherit and perceive, just as "I" do, its own causally determined nature. Cf. note 65 (Buddhism).

T.W. Rhys Davids, *Dial.* II.43, ŚBE XXXVI.142. Mil. 48 B.C. Law, *Concepts of Buddhism,* 1937, p. 45—"It goes without saying that the Buddhist thinker repudiates the notion of the passing of the ego from one embodiment to another".

Takakusu, *Philosophy East and West,* 1944, pp. 78-9. "The idea is not that a soul lives after the death of the body and moves into another body. Samsara means the creation of a new life by the influence of the actions of the former living being".

Petavatthu IV.3 Peta confesses false doctrine held as a man, viz., that "just as he who leaves one village finds his way into another, even so does the living being enter another body". Cf. Mil.72.

[76]M.I.256f.; Mil.72 *n'atthi koci satto yo imamhā kāyā aññaṁ kāyam saṅkamati.* Cf. note 63 (Buddhism).

[77]S.II.95, cf. notes 63, 64 (Buddhism).

another? Thus the Vedanta and Buddhism are in complete agreement that while there is transmigration, there are no individual transmigrants. All that we see is the operation of causes, and so much the worse for us if we see in this fatally determined nexus our "Self ". We can find the same thing in Christianity, where it is asked, "Who did sin, this man or his parents, that he was born blind?" to which the remarkable answer is made that "Neither hath this man sinned, nor his parents: but that the works of God might be made manifest in him".[78] In otherwords, the blindness has "arisen" by the operation of those mediate causes of which God is the First Cause and without which the world would have been deprived of the perfection of causality.[79]

The Buddha's purpose is to save us from our selves and their mortality. He would go on to say that our subjection to such fatal accidents as blindness is a part and parcel of our identification of "consciousness" with "Self ". We altogether misunderstand the value and importance of "consciousness";[80] "that is not my Self "; and the Parable of the Raft applies as much to consciousness as to ethical procedure; like the raft, consciousness is a

[78]John IX.2-3.

[79]Fortune is nothing but the series or order of second causes, and lies in these causes themselves and not in God (except Providentially, i.e. in the same way that the Buddha "knows whatever is to be known, as it has been and will be", Sn. 558, etc., cf. Pras.Up.IV.5) who does not govern directly but through these causes, with which he never interferes (St. Thomas Aquinas, *Sum. Theol.*, I.22-3, I.103.7 ad 2, I.116.2, 4 etc.). "Nothing happens in the world by chance". Leveippus Aehos.I.25.4 (in Burnet). Timaeus, 28A-Cf. St. Augustine, QQ LXXXIII.qu.24; Timaeus 28a. "As a mother is pregnant with unborn offspring, so is the world itself with the causes of unborn things" (*De Trin.*III.9,—both statements endorsed by St. Thomas Aquinas). "Why then should miserable men venture to pride themselves on their freewill before they are set free?" (St Augustine, *De spir. et lit.*, 52). The Buddha clearly demonstrates that we can neither be as nor when we will, and are not free (S.III.66, 67), though "there is a Way" (D.I.156) to become so. It is the grasp of the very fact that "we" are mechanisms, causally determined (as stated in the repeated formula, "This being so, that arises; or not being so, does not arise")—the very ground of "scientific materialism"—that points out the Way of escape; all our trouble arises from the fact that like Boethius we have "forgotten who we are", and ignorantly see our Self in-what-is-not-our-Self (*anattani attānam*), but only a process.

Further References: Plato, *Timaeus* 28a;

Aristotle, *Metaphysics* VI.3.1 (1027 a)—"Will A be or not? It will if B happens; otherwise not. And B will happen if C does. It is clear that in this way, as time is continuously subtracted from a limited period, we shall come to the present".

Renner, *Psychologia* (p. 245), will = freewill—both passive reactions in us; will = want.

St. Thomas Aquinas I.26.1 and II.11.25.7—"The will is free insofar as it obeys reason"—not when we "do what we like". I.20.1—distinction of *will* from *wanting*, sensitive *appetite* (= passions).

Shams-i-Tabrīz XIII—"Whoso hath not escaped free will, no will hath he".

Philo, *Conf.* 94.

[80]As "conscious" we are always "conscious subjects" rather than substances—that which *underlies* or *understands* consciousness.

valuable tool, a means of operation, but like the raft not to be held on to when the work has been done.[81] If this alarms us, as Aristha was frightened because he thought that the peace of Nirvāṇa implied a destruction of something real in himself,[82] we must not overlook that what we are asked to substitute for our consciousness of things pleasant and unpleasant—or rather, subjection to feelings of pleasure and pain—is not a simple *un*consciousness but a superconsciousness, none the less real and beatific because it cannot be analysed in the terms of conscious thought. At the same time we ought, perhaps, to point out that this superconsciousness,or what in Christian theology is called the "divine manner of knowing, not by means of any objects external to the knower", is by no means to be equated with the *sub*consciousness of modern psychology, with respect to which it has been very truly said that while "nineteenth century materialism closed the mind of man to what is above him, twentieth century psychology open it to what is below him".[83]

Our conscious "life" is a process, subject to corruption and death. It is this life that must be "*arrested*" (*nirodho*) if we are to live immortally. It will be useless to deal with symptoms; it is the cause or occasion (*hetu, nidāna*) that must be sought if we are to find the "medecine" that the Buddha sought and found. It is the understanding of things "as become" (*Yathā bhūtam*), and the realisation that "personality" (*ātmabhāva*) is one of these things, that liberates man from himself. The gist of the Buddhist gospel is resumed in the often and triumphant repeated words,

Of all things that spring from a cause,
  The cause has been told by him "Thus-come";
And their suppression, too,
  The Great Pilgrim has declared.

[81]M.I.261 *nittharaṇatthāya na gahaṇatthāya.* Cf. note 106 (Buddhism).

[82]Axiochus feared "unconsciousness" with such a state (Cf. Axiochus 370, 226a); Maitreyi was benitered by the words of Yājñavalkya-*na pretya sanjñā'sti* (BU.II.4.12).

Cf. S.III.105—Yamaka's heresy that 'liberated' meant 'annihilated', but *diṭṭh'eva dhamma, tathāgaṭa,* is not *saccalo thethato* and is *anupalabhiyamāno* now, how much more so post mortem. S.II.116f.—neither *hoti* nor *nahoti* nor any combination of these. M.I.137, 140 "Naughtily, vainly, falsely, and against the fact am I charged with being a misleader and a teacher of the cutting off, destruction and non-entity of what really is" (*sato satassa* = *to ontōs on* = real being); there is here a play on the double meaning of the word *venayika,* (1) leader-away, destroyer (e.g. of the Ego-heresy, but not of what "really is") and (2) leader forth, guide, as in M.I.386 similarly S.III.110f. Cf. BU.IV.5.1 (Maitreyi's fear); KU.I.20-2 (even the Gods had doubt of this, "Is, or is not", after passing over); CU.VIII.5.3, VIII.9.1. "Yet it would be improper to say even of a Buddha after death that 'He knows not, he sees not'" (D.II.68). His nature cannot be expressed by any antithesis or combination of the terms "Is" or "Is not". He "is", but not in any "place" (Mil. 73). Also, like *Migr.* 183 He "shows nowhere—cannot be pointed out". *Adeiktos* (not shown) corresponds to A.A.III.2.4 *anādiṣtaḥ.*

[83]Rene Guenon, "L'Erreur du psychologisme", *Etudes Traditionelles,* 43, 1938. "The most evil type of man is he who, in his waking hours, has the qualities we found in his dream state". (Plato, *Republic,* 567B).

In this chain of causes, to understand which is to have come Awake, it is emphasised that nothing whatever happens by chance but only in a regular sequence—"That being present, this becomes; that not being present, this does not become".[84] To have verified this is to have found the Way. For in "all things that spring from a cause" are included "old age, sickness, and death"; and when we know the cause, we can apply the cure. The applicated is stated in the cycle of "causal origination" mastered on the night of the Great Awakening. All the ills that flesh is heir to are inseparable from and essential to the process of existence and unavoidable by any individual; individuality is "consciousness"; consciousness is not a being, but a passion, not an activity but only a sequence of reactions in which "we", who have no power to be either as or when we will, are fatally involved; individuality is motivated by and perpetuated by wanting; and the cause of all wanting is "ignorance" (*avidyā*),—for we "ignore" that the objects of our desire can never be possessed in any real sense of the word, ignore that even when we have got what we want, we still "want" to keep it and are still "in want". The ignorance meant is of things as they really are (*yathā bhūtam*), and the consequent attribution of substantiality to what is merely phenomenal; the seeing of Self in what is not-Self.[85]

In making ignorance the root of all evil, Buddhism concurs with all traditional doctrine.[86] But we must guard ourselves from supposing that an ignorance of any particular thing is meant, and especially against a confusion of the traditional "ignorance" with what we mean by "illiteracy"; so far from this, our empirical knowledge of facts is an essential part of the very ignorance that makes desire possible. And no less must another misunderstanding be avoided; we must not suppose that the traditional wisdom is opposed to the knowledge of useful facts; what it demands is that we should recognize in what are called "facts" and "laws of science", not absolute truths but statements of

[84]M.II.32; S.II.28 and passim. Cf. Aristotle, Metaphysics VI.3.2 Philo, Aet. 28, 35, 74.

[85]S.III.162.164, etc. "Ignorance" is failure to distinguish body-and-consciousness from Self.

Plato, *Apology* 29 B to *gar agnoe* in = ignorance; *Laws* 689 The vice of the Soul is ignorance, its virtue is Knowledge—(Hermes Lib.X.8, 9). Ignorance is the failure to distinguish body-andconsciousness, self from Self.

[86]Philo, *Elr.* 160, *ignoia* (ignorance) is the cause of all sin. A.IV.195, Dh. 243, *avijjā param malam*; cf. M.I.263, S.III.171 *avijjā, vijjā* defined; S.IV.256 *avijjā* defined as of origin, cessation and way to arrest *dukkha*. With D.I.70 on the infatuation that results from the indulgence of vision and other senses, cf. Plato, *Protagoras*, 356D, "It is the power of appearance (*to phainomenon* = Pali *rūpa*) that leads us astray", 357E "To be overcome by pleasure is ignorance in the highest degree", 358C. "This yielding to oneself is just 'ignorance' and just as surely is mastery of oneself 'wisdom'" (*sophia* = Pali *kusalatā, hochmā*); the medicine for ignorance being "knowledge" (*episteme*), *Critias* 106B. Similarly Hermes *Lib.* X.8.9. "The voice of the soul is ignorance, its virtue knowledge", *Lib.* XIII.7B where "ignorance" is the first of the "twelve torments of matter" (as in the Buddhist Chain of Causes, cf. Hartmann in JAOS. 60, 1940, 356-60), and *Lib.* I.18. "The cause of death is desire", implying the choice between opposites.

statistical probability. The pursuit of scientific knowledge does not necessarily imply an "ignorance"; it is only when the motive is a curiosity, only when we pursue knowledge for its own sake, or art for art's sake, that we are behaving "ignorantly".[87] In Brāhmaṇical terms, "ignorance" is of who we are; in Buddhist language, of what we are not; and these are only two ways of saying the same thing, what we really are being definable only in terms of what we are not.

It is only by making stepping stones of our dead selves, until we realise at last that there is literally nothing with which we can identify our Self, that we can become what we are. And hence the Buddhist emphasis on what in Christian terms is called "selfnaughting", an expression based on Christ's *denegat seipsum.* "Behold the Arhat's beatitude! No wanting can be found in them; excised the thought 'I am'; unmoving, unoriginated, uncontaminated, very Persons, God—become (*brahma-bhūtā*), great heroes, natural sons of the Wake; unshaken in whatever plight, released from further becoming (*punar bhava*), on ground of dompted-self they stand, they in the world have won their battle; they roar the 'Lion's roar'; incomparable are the Wake" (*buddhāḥ*)[88]. There is no question here of a post mortem deliverance, but of "Persons" triumphant here and now; nor will it be overlooked that the epithet "Buddha" is used in the plural, and applied to all who have reached their goal.

Of such it is often said that they are "despirated" (*nirvāta*). The word Nirvāṇa, "despiration", which plays so large a part in our conception of Buddhism, where it is one of the most important of the many terms that are the referents to "man's last end", demands some further explanation. The verb nirvā is, literally, to "blow out", not transitively, but as a fire ceases to draw, i.e. "draw breath".[89] The older texts employ the nearly synonymous verb *udvā,* to "blow out" or "go out";[90] "when the Fire blows out (*udvāyati*) it is into the Gale that it expires";[91] deprived of fuel, the fire of life is "pacified",

[87]Cicero *Academica* 11.29 where Antiochus (academician) says, "no man could be a sage (*sapiens*) who was ignorant of either the beginning of knowledge or the end of appetition, and who therefore know not from what he was starting or at what he ought to arrive".

Xenophon, *The Memorabilia* of Socrates I.6.10 "*egō de nomizdō to men deisthai theion einai, to d'hōs elachistōn engutatō tou theiou*" = I think in the first place that it is necessary to be god-like, but at any rate to be as near as possible to the divine.

[88]S.III.83, 84.

[89]In AB.III.4 Agni, when he "draws and burns" (*pravān dahati*) is identified with Vāyu. In KB.VII.9 the Breaths "blow" (*vānti*) in various directions, but "do not blow out" (*na nirvanti*). In JUB.IV.12.6 "Agni, becoming the Breath, shines" (*prāṇo bhūtvā agnir dīpyate*). In RV.X.129.2 *ānīd avātam,* "not blowing" is very near in meaning to *nirvātam* (*ānīd avātam* corresponding to Meister Eckhart's *gegeistet* und *engeistet,* "equally spirated, despirated"). Cf. BU.III.8.8 *avāyu . . . aprāṇa.* The word *nirvāṇa* does not occur in the Brāhmaṇical literature before *Bhagavad Gītā.*

[90]TS.II.2.4.7 *udvāyet,* "if the fire goes out"; KB.VII.2 *udvāte'nagnau* "in what is not fire, but gone out".

[91]CU.IV.3.1 *yadā-agnir udvāyati vāyume vāpyeti.* In having thus "gone to the wind" the fire has "gone home" (JUB.III.1.17). Cf. note 166 (Buddhism).

i.e. quenched,[92] when the mind has been curbed, one attains to the "peace of Nirvāṇa", despiration in God".[93] In the same way Buddhism stresses the going out of the fire or light of life for want of fuel;[94] it is by ceasing to feed our fires that the peace is reached, of which it is well said in another tradition that "it passeth understanding"; our present life is a continuity of coming to be and passing away and immediate rebirth, like a flame that goes on burning and is not the same nor yet another flame; and in the same way with rebirth after death, it is like the lighting of one flame from another; nothing concrete passes over, there is continuity, but not sameness.[95] But "the contemplatives go out like this lamp" which, once out, "cannot pass on its flame".[96] Nirvāṇa is a kind of death, but like every death a rebirth to something other than what had been. *Pari* in *parinirvāṇa* merely adds the value "complete" to the notion of a despiration.[97]

We say "a kind of death" because the word *nirvāṇa* can be used of still living things. The Bodhisattva is "despirated" when he becomes the Buddha. Even more significant, we find that each of the stages completed in the training of a royal steed is called a Parinirvāṇa.[98] The Buddha uses the word chiefly in connection with the "quenching" of the fires of passion, fault and delusion (*rāga, doṣa* and *moha*). But there is a distinction involved here; the despiration is a present (*saṁdṛṣṭikam*) experience in two ways, ethical in as much as it implies the eradication of passion and fault, and eternal, i.e. metaphysical, in that it is a liberation from delusion, or ignorance (*avidyā*); from both points of view it involves an unselfishness, but on the one hand in practise, on the other in theory.[99] Thus while the denotation is that of the Greek *aposbennumi* (be still, go out, be quenched, of wind, fire or passion), the connotation is that of Greek *teleō* and *teleutaō* (to be perfected, to die). All these meanings can be resumed in the one English word "finish"; the finished product is no longer in the making, no longer *becoming* what it ought to be; in the same way the finished being, the perfected man has done with all becoming; the final

[92]Pras.Up.III.9; MU.VI.34.

[93]BG.VI.15; BG.II.72 *brahma-nirvāṇam ṛcchati.*

[94]M.I.487, etc., and as in MU.VI.34.1. Cf. *Rūmī Mathnawī* I.3705.

[95]Mil. 40, 47, 71.72.

[96]Sn. 135 *nibbantī dhīrā yathā yam padīpo* (deictic). Cf. Th.2.116; Sn. 19 *vivatā kuṭi, nibbuto gini.* "Man, like a light in the night, is kindled and put out" (Heracleitus, Fr. LXXVII).

[97]S.V.282 (*akiṁcano pandito hīṇasāvā*) *te loke parinibbūta.*

[98]M.I.446.

[99]A.I.156 In the series *rago, doso* and *moho, moho* (delusion) can be replaced by its equivalent *avijjā*, ignorance (e.g. *Itivuttaka*, 57) and it will be the more readily seen that freedom from *rāgo* and *doso* is a moral virtue, and freedom from *moho* = *avijjā* an intellectual virtue.

In nearly the same way *Itivuttaka* 38, 39 distinguishes between the two Nibbanas, (1) present, with some residue of the factors of existence, and (2) ultimate, without any residue of factors of existence. This, also, marks the distinction of Nibbāna from Parinibbāna, so far as this can be really made.

dissolution of the body cannot affect him, however affecting it may be to others, themselves imperfect, unfinished. Nirvāṇa is a final end, and like Brahma, a matter about which no further questions can be asked by those who are still on fire.[100]

In other words, the Way involves on the one hand a practical and on the other a contemplative discipline. The contemplative corresponds to the athlete, who does not contest for the prize unless he is already "in training". When the Indians speak of the Comprehensor (*evamvit*) of a given doctrine, they do not mean by this merely one who grasps the logical significance of a given proposition; they mean one who has "verified" it in his own person, and is what he knows; for so long as we know only of our immortal Self, we are still in the realm of ignorance; we only really know it when we become it; we cannot really know it without being it. There are ways of life dispositive to such a realisation, and other ways that must prevent it. Let us, therefore, pause to consider the nature of the "mere morality", or as it is now called, "Ethics", apart from which the contemplative life would be impossible. What we should call a "practical holiness" is called alike in the old Indian books and in Buddhism a present and timeless "Walking with God" (*brahmacarya*).[101] But there is also a clear distinction of the Doctrine (*dharma*) from its practical Meaning (*artha*), and it is with the latter that we are for the moment concerned.

In agreement with the old Indian theory of the relation of the Regnum to the Sacerdotium, we find a Buddhist king who requests the Bodhisattva to give him instruction both in Ethics (*artha*) and in Doctrine (*dharma*),[102] and this context will enable us to grasp the distinction very clearly. We find that Ethics is a matter of liberality (*dāna*) and of commandments (*Śīla*). More in detail, the king is to provide for all his subjects' needs, and to make honourable provision for both men and animals when superannuated and no longer able to do what they did in their prime. On the other hand, the whole of what is here called the Doctrine is stated in the form of the "chariot simile", of which more later.

The terms "commandments" demands a further analysis. These rules of what is sometimes styled "mere morality"—"mere" because although indispensable—if we are to reach man's last end, morality is not in itself an end, but only a means—are not quite rigidly fixed; in general, the reference is to the "five" or "ten virtuous habits". As five, these are (1) not to kill, (2) not to steal, (3) not to follow the lusts of the flesh, (4) to refrain from lying, and (5) to refrain from the use of intoxicants. These are essential preliminaries for any spiritual development, and are expected of all laymen. The set of ten includes the first four of the five, and (5) to avoid slander, (6) to refrain from abusive speech, (7) to avoid frivolous converse, (8) not to covet, (9) not to

[100]M.I.304; S.III.188. Cf. BU.III.6 (Brahma). Cf. James III.6.

[101]Sn. 567 *brahmacariyaṁ saṁdiṭṭhikam akālikam.* Cf. AV.XI.5; CU.VIII.5.

[102]J.VI.251/2. *Dharma* is "Law of Nature", *svadharma* is law of Nature in its distributive aspect.

bear malice, and (10) to entertain no false views. The last has particular reference to the avoidance of heresies such as the belief in "soul", the view that causal determination cancels moral responsibility, the view that there is "no other world", the view that the Buddha has taught a novel doctrine, the view that he teaches an annihilation or cutting off of anything but sorrow. The foregoing five or ten rules are to be distinguished from the five or ten "bases of training" of the monastic rule; the first five of these are the same as the five already listed, to which are added (6) not to eat at irregular hours, (7) not to attend musical and theatrical performances, (8) to refrain from the use of unguents and ornaments, (9) not to sleep on luxurious beds, and (10) not to accept gold or silver.[103]

Before we return to the Doctrine we must carefully guard ourselves from thinking that the Buddha attaches an absolute value to moral conduct. We must not, for example, suppose that because the means are partly ethical, Nirvāṇa is therefore an ethical state. So far from this, un-self-ishness, from the Indian point of view is an amoral state, in which no question of "altruism" can present itself, liberation being as much from the notion of "others" as it is from the notion of "self ";[104] and not in any sense a psychological state, but a liberation from all that is implied by the "psyche" in the word "psychology". "I call him a Brāhmaṇa indeed", the Buddha says, "who has passed beyond attachment both to good and evil; one who is clean, to whom no dust attaches, a-pathetic".[105] In the well known Parable of the Raft (of ethical procedure) by means of which one crosses the river of life, he asks very pointedly "what does a man do with the boat when he has reached the other side of the river? Does he carry it about on his back, or does he leave it on the shore?"[106] Perfection is something more than an infantile innocence; there must be knowledge of what are folly and wisdom, good and evil, and of how to be rid of *both* these values, and of how to be "right without being righteous", "moral amorally"

[103]PTS. Pali Dic., s.v.*sīlā*. In greater detail M.I.179, 180 and in A.11.

[104]*Udāna* 70.

[105]Dh. 412; cf. Sn. 363, Mil.383 and next Note. "Apathetic", i.e. "not pathological", as are those who are subject to their own passions or sym-pathise with those of others. Note *karuṇā*, 'pity' does not imply sym-*pathy*.

[106]M.I.135; like the raft, "right is to be abandoned, and a fortiori wrong". "I need no further rafts" (Sn. 21). Cf. Dh. 39, 267, 412; Sn. 4, 547; M.II.26, 27: TB.III.12.9.8; BG.II.50; Kaus.Up.III.8; KU.II.14; Mund.Up.III.1.3; MU.VI.18, etc.; Meister Eckhart, passim.

Similarly St. Augustine, *De Spir. et Lit.*, 16, "Let him no longer use the Law as a means of arrival when he has arrived"; St. Augustine, *Contra Acad.* III.2; Meister Eckhart, "If I intend to cross the sea and want a ship, that is part and parcel of wanting to be over, and having gotten to the otherside I do not want a ship" (Evans II.194). In the same way the discriminating consciousness (*viññānam* = *saññā*, S.III.140, 142 = *saṁjñā*, BU.II.4.12 and wholly inferior to *paññā, prajñā*) is a very useful means of crossing over, but nothing to hold on to thereafter (M.I.260, see note 81 (Buddhism)). "Consciousness" is a kind of "ignorance", ceasing at our death (BU.IV.4.3); accordingly *avidyayā mṛtyuṁ tīrtvā, vidyayā'mṛtam aśnute* (Īśā.Up.11; MU.VII.9).

(*sīlavat no ca sīlamayaḥ*, M.II.27; Eckhart—"... she would not merely practise virtues, but virtue as a whole would be her life ...", Evans trans. Vol. I, p. 374). For the Arhat, having "done all that was to be done" (*kṛta-karaṇīyam*), there is nothing more that should be done (BG.III.17 *kāryam na vidyate*), and therefore no possibility of merit or demerit; injunctions and prohibitions have no longer any meaning where there is no longer anything that ought or ought not to be done. For there indeed, as Meister Eckhart says of the Kingdom of God, "neither vice nor virtue ever entered it"; just as in the Upanishad, where neither vice nor virtue can pass over the Bridge of Immortality.[107] The Arhat is "no longer under the Law"; he is "not under the Law",[108] but a "Mover-at-will" and a "Doer of what he will"; if *we* find that he acts unselfishly in our ethical sense of the word, that is our interpretation, for which he is not responsible. Only the Patripassian and Monophysite can offer any objection to the points of view.

It must also be clearly realised that it will be convenient at this point to ask, "*Who* is the Wake?"[109] For the answer to this question will tell us as much as can be told of those who have followed in his footsteps to the end, and can be spoken of as "World-enders" (*lokantagu*). Who is the Great Person, the Kinsman of the Sun, the Eye in the World,[110] the descendant of Angirasa, the God of Gods, who says of himself that he is neither a God, nor a Genius nor a man, but a Buddha, one in whom all the conditions that determine particular modes of existence have been destroyed.[111] What are these Arhats, who like the Vedic immortals, have won to being what they are by their "dignity"?

The question can be approached from many different angles. In the first place, the Buddha's names and epithets are suggestive; in the Vedas, for example, the first and most of Aṅgirases are Agni and Indra,[112] to whom also the designation of "Arhat" is oftenest applied. Agni is, like the Buddha, "awakened at dawn" (*uṣarbudh*): Indra is urged to be "of waking mind" (*bodhin-manas*),[113] and when overcome by pride in his own strength he actually "awakens" himself when reproached by his spiritual alter-ego.[114] That

[107]CU.VIII.4.1, etc. Meister Eckhart, "There neither vice nor virtue ever entered in".

[108]Galatians V.18.

[109]It will be seen that this is, strictly speaking, an improper question; a Buddha is no longer anyone.

[110]Cf. TS.II.9.3, II.3.8.1,2. The expression "Eye in the World" amounts to an equation of the Buddha with Agni and the Sun.

[111]A.II.37.

[112]RV.I.31.1 (Agni), I.130.3 (Indra).

[113]RV.V.75.5 (in order that he may overcome Vṛtra). *Bodhin-manas* suggests the Buddhist *bodhi-citta*. Mil. 75 assimilates *buddhi*, Buddha.

[114]BD.VII.57 *sa* (Indra) *buddhvā ātmānam.* RV.V.30.2 *indram naro bubudhānā aśema.* Contrast RV.VIII.70.3 *nakiṣtam karmaṇā naśat ... na yajñaiḥ.*

The Jātaka tales include many of the Buddha's former births as Sakka (Indra). In the Nikāyas Sakka acts as the Buddha's protector, just as Indra acts for Agni; but it is

the Buddha is called "Great Person" and "Most Man" (*mahā puruṣa, nṛtama*) by no means tells us that he is "a man", since these are epithets of the highest Gods in the oldest Brāhmaṇical books. Māyā is not a woman's name, but Natura naturans, our "Mother Nature".[115] Or if we consider the miraculous life, we shall find that almost every detail, from the free choice of the time and place of birth[116] to the lateral birth itself[117] and the taking of the Seven

---

the Buddha himself that overcomes Māra. In other words, the Buddha is comparable to that Agni who is "both Agni and Indra, *brahma* and *kṣatra*". In M.I.386 the Buddha seems to be addressed as Indra (*purindado sakko*); but elsewhere, e.g. Sn. 1069 and when his disciples are called sakya-puttiyo, "sons of the Sakyan", the reference is to the Sakya clan, whose name like Indra's implies a "being able".

[115]*Māyā* (the "means" of all creation, divine or human, or "art" by which anything is made), is "magic" in the sense of Behmen, *Sex Puncta Mystica*, V.1.f.—("The Mother of eternity; the original state of Nature; the formative power in the eternal wisdom, the power of imagination, a mother in all three worlds; of use to the children of God's kingdom, and to the sorcerers for the devil's kingdom; for the understanding can make of it what it pleases").

Māyā for Śaṅkaracārya—the greatest exponent of *māyāvāda*—is "the Unrevealed, the Power (*śakti*) of the Lord, the beginningless Unknowable (*avidyā*), inferable by the wise in relation to what-can-be-made (*kārya* = *factibilia*), ["Man therefore knows not, or his appetites Their first affections"—Dante, *Purgatory* XVIII.52] that by which all this moving—world is brought to birth . . . -and by whom are both Bondage and Liberation effected".—*Vivekachudāmani* 108, 569.

In such contexts as this the gerundive *avidyā*, synonymous with "Power", cannot be simply "Ignorance" but is much rather "mystery" or "opinion" as opposed to *vidyā*, "what can be known" : *avidyā* is a Potentiality that can only be known by its effects, by all that is *māyāmaya*. Māyā is the *Nature* of God. Māyā, in other words, is the Theotokos and mother of all living. Other parallels: Metis, the mother of Athena; Sophia; Kausalya the mother of Rama; as Maia was the mother of Hermes, Hesiod, *Theog.* 938). Of whom else could the Buddha have been born? That the mothers of Bodhisattvas die young is really because as Heracleitus says (Fr.X), "Nature loves to hide". Māyā "vanishes" just as Urvaśī, mother of Āyuś (Agni) by Purūravas, vanished, and as Saraṇyū vanished from Vivasvān; Māyā's *svamūrti* Pajāpati taking her place (BC.I.18; II.19, 20) as Saraṇyū's *savarṇā* took hers. The eternal Avatāra has, indeed, always "two mothers", eternal and temporal, sacerdotal and royal. See also my "Nirmāṇakāya", JRAS, 1938. Māyā, being the "art" by which all things or any thing is made (*nirmita*, "measured out"), and "art" having been originally a mysterious and magical knowledge, acquires its other and pejorative sense (e.g. MU.IV.2) in the same way that art, artifice, craft, cunning and sleight, are not only virtues essential to the maker by art (*artifex*), but can also imply artfulness, artificiality (falsity), craftiness, guile and trickery; it is the bad sense, for example that "Consciousness is a glamour" (*māyā viya viññānam*, Vis. 479, S.III.142), while on the other hand Wycliff could still render our "wise as serpents" (Matth.X.16, cf. RV.VI.52.15, *ahimāyāḥ*) by "sly as serpents". Cf. Betty Heimann, *Māyā in Indian and Western Philosophy*, pp. 49f.

[116]Cf. JUB.III.28.4, *yadi brāhmaṇa-kule yadi rāja-kule*, like J.I.49, *khattiya-kule vā brāhmaṇa-kule*.

[117]RV.IV.18.2 (Indra) *pārśvat nirgamāṇi*; BC.I.25 (Buddha) *pārśvat sutaḥ*. So too both Agni (RV.VI.16.35 *garbhe mātuḥ—vididyutānaḥ*) and the Buddha (D.II.13 *kucchigatam passati*) are visible in the womb. Many other parallels could be drawn.

Strides,[118] and from the Going Forth to the Great Awakening on the strewn altar at the foot of the World-tree at the Navel of the Earth, and from the defeat of the Dragons to the miraculous kindling of the sacrificial firewood,[119] can be exactly paralleled—and in saying "exactly" we mean just that—in the Vedic mythology of Agni and Indra, priest and king *indivinis.* For example, and the single instance must suffice, if the Vedic Dragon fights with fire and smoke,[120] and also with women for weapons,[121] so does Māra, Death, whom the Buddhist texts still refer to as "Holdfast"; if the Vedic Dragonslayer is deserted by the Gods and must rely upon his own resources, so is the Bodhisattva left alone, and can only call upon his own powers to assist him.[122] In saying this we do not mean to deny that the Buddha's defeat of Māra is an allegory of self-conquest, but only to point out that this is a very old story, one that has always and everywhere been told; and that in its Buddhist setting the story is not a new one, but derived immediately from the Vedic tradition, where the same story is told, and where it has the same significance.[123]

That the perfected possess the power of motion and manifestation at will is familiar in Christian teaching, where they "shall pass in and out and find pasture";[124] and such powers are naturally proper to those who, being "joined unto the Lord, are one spirit".[125] The like is repeatedly enunciated in the Brāhmaṇical scriptures, and often in nearly the same words. In an often recurring context the Buddha describes the four stages of contemplation (*dhyāna*) of paths of power (*ṛddhipāda*) that are the equivalent of the "Aryan Path" and are means to Omniscience, Full Awakening and Nirvāṇa.[126] When

[118]RV.X.8.4 (Agni) *sapta dadhiṣe padāni,* X.122.3 (Agni) *sapta dhāmāni pariyan;* J.I.53 (Bodhisattva) *satta-pada-vītihārena agamāsi.*

[119]TS.II.5.8.3; cf. I Kings 18.38.

[120]RV.I.32.13.

[121]RV.V.30.9, X.27.10.

[122]RV.VIII.96.7; AB.III.20; Sn. 425f Namuci = Māra = Pāpimā = *dummano* Yakkha. Namuci is called a "royal serpent" (*sarparāja*), S.I.106. S.B.XI.1.5.7 "... he thus slays sin, Vṛtra, which ever keeps him from well-being, from virtue, and from the good work: ... ". ŚB.XII.7.3.4 "... Namuci is evil: having thus, indeed, slain that evil, his hateful enemy, Indra wrest from him his energy, or vital power".

[123]Cf. RV.III.51.3 where Indra, elsewhere *vṛtra-han,* etc., is *abhimāti-han,* similarly RV.IX.65.15 and passim. *Abhimati* (= *abhimāna,* MU.VI.28, i.e. *asmi-māna*), the Ego-notion, is already the Enemy, the Dragon to be overcome. References from the Rg Veda :

III.53.8; III.61.7-8 and V.63.4 Mitra-Varuṇa; V.2.1 Agni's; V.31.7 Indra's; V.40.6,8 Svarbhānu's; III.20.3 Agni; VI.18.9 Vṛtra's; VI.20.4 Susna's; VI.22.9; VI.44.22 Māyāh of Soma overcome by Indu (Tvaṣṭṛ vada); VII.98.5 overcome by Indra in using Soma; X.54.4 Indra's wars = *māyā;* X.53.9 *Tvaṣṭā māyā vet.* ...

[124]John X.9, 14; *Purgatory* XXVII.131. Cf. SA.VII.22; Taitt.Up.III.10.5.

[125]I Cor.6.17.

[126]S.II.212f., V.254f., A.I.170, I.254f., etc.

Iddhi (Skr. *ṛddhi,* from *ṛddh,* to prosper, *emporwachsen*) is virtue, power (in the sense of Mark V.30 *dunamis* = power), art (e.g. skill of a hunter, M.I.152), talent or gift. The

all these stations of contemplation (*dhyāna*) have been so mastered that the practitioner can pass from one to another at will, and similarly commands the composure or synthesis (*samādhi*) to which they lead, then in this state of unification (*eko'vadhi-bhāva*) the liberated Arhat is at once omniscient and omnipotent; the Buddha, describing his own attainment, can remember his "former habitations" (*pūrva-nivāsa*), or as we should be apt to say, "past births", in every detail; and describing his powers (*ṛddhi*), he says that "I, brethren, can realise (*pratyanubhū*) whatever countless powers I will; being many, I become one, and having been many become also one;[127] seen or unseen, I can pass through a wall or a mountain as if it were air; I can sink into the earth or emerge from it as though it were water; I can walk on the water as if it were solid earth;[128] I can move through the air like a bird; I can touch

---

iddhis of the Iddhi-pāda, "Footing of Power", are super-normal rather than abnormal. We cannot take up here at any length the apparent difficulty presented by the fact that *iddhis* are also attributed to the Buddha's Adversary (Māra, Namuci, Ahi-Nāga), except to point out that "Death" is also (in the same sense that Satan remains an "angel") a spiritual being and the "powers" are not in themselves moral, but much rather intellectual virtues. (Cf. *Pratyāhāra* in Śaṅkaracārya's *Aparokshānubhuti*-103, 121.) The Buddha's powers are greater than the Adversary's because his range is greater; he knows the Brahmaloka as well as the worlds up to the Brahmaloka (i.e. under the Sun), while "Death's" power extends only up to the Brahmaloka and not beyond the Sun. (*The Gospel of Sri Ramakrishna,* 1944, p. 26.)

On levitation and *iddhis* generally, see S.V.252f., 282, 283. The prerequisites for such powers are *chanda-samādhi-pradhāna-sankhāra-samaññāgatam.* S.V.252, 291—where *iddhi pāda* tends, conduces to "neither shore", but to *nibbāna.* A.IV.333 opposite of *viriya* as above is inertia, thinking *me kāyo garuko akammañño,* and therefore lying down, not employing heroic effort of will. Vis. 144—because of *ubbeyāpīti,* Mahāvissa *ākāse langhā pana ppamāṇa hoti* (causative).

Dh. A IV.118 Vakkali's balavapīti enables him to fly through the air. J.II.111 mentions the same cause for walking on water. The Homeric hero disappears by being clothed with air.

See also *Timaeus* 42C; Vis. 143-4 and Dh A.IV.118f. = Curtaha result of pīti, delight, transport. *Svayam* = *agurutva.*

[127] *Timaeus* 68D—To be able to blend many into one and again dissolve one into many is God's power alone.

[128] For the earlier history of levitation and such powers see W.N. Brown, *Walking on the Water,* Chicago, 1928, pp.13-18. This is primarily the power of the Spirit (Genesis, I.2). It is typically of the unseen Gale (Vāyu) of the Spirit that motion at will is predicated (RV.X.168.4 *ātmā devānām—yathā vaśaṁ carati—na rūpaṃ tasmai*). In AV.X.7.38 the primal Yakṣa (Brahma) "strides" upon the ridge of the sea; and so, accordingly, the brahmacārī, ib.XI.5.26, for "Even as Brahma can change his form and move at will, so amongst all beings can he (the *brahma-bhūta*) change his form and move at will who is a Comprehensor thereof" (SA.VII.22); "The One God (Indra) stands upon the flowing streams at will" (AV.III.13.4, TS.V.6.1.3). "Self-motion (*to auto chinoun*) is the very word and essence of the Soul" (cf. *Phaedrus* 245).

This is like all other forms of *levi*-tation, a matter of *light*ness. Thus in S.I.1 the Buddha "crossed the flood only when I did not support myself or make any effort"

with my hands the sun and moon; I have power with respect to my body even so far as unto the Brahma-world".[129] The same powers are exercised by other adepts to the extent that they have perfected themselves in the same disciplines and are masters of composure (*samādhi*); it is only when contemplation (*dhyāna*) fails that the power of motion-at-will is lost.[130] The Buddha employs the old Brahmanical formula[131] when he says that he has taught his disciples to extract from this material body another body of intellectual substance (*manomaya kāya*), as one might draw an arrow from its sheath, a sword from its scabbard, or a snake from its slough; it is with this

---

(*appatittham anāyūham ogham atari*); i.e. not bearing down upon the surface of the water; Cf. P. Arunachalam "*Studies and Translations*" p. 50; St. Augustine, *Confessions* XIII.4—"Thy Good Spirit moved upon the waters, yet was not born up by the waters, as if he found rest in them".

Mil. 84, 85 explains the power of travelling through the air, "even to the Brahma-world", as like that of one who jumps (*langhayati*), resolving (*cittam uppādeti*) "There will I alight", with which intention his "body grows light" (*kāyo me lahuko hoti*), and it is similarly "by the power of thought" (*citta-vasena*) that one moves through the air. (BSOS. VI.885). Lightness (*laghutva*) is developed by contemplation (Śvet.Up.II.13; *Yogasūtra* III.42-3; *Theragāthā* 104), all the powers (*iddhi*) are resultants of contemplations (*jhāna*, cf. note 129 (Buddhism)) and depend upon it, so that it can be asked "who sinks not in the gulf without support or stay?" and answered "One who is prescient, fully synthesised (*susamāhito*), he may cross the flood so hard to pass" (ogham tarati duttaram, S.I.53, where the application is ethical). The notion of "lightness" underlies the ubiquitous symbolism of "birds" and "wings" (RV.VI.9.5; PB.V.3.5, XIV.1.13, XXV.3.4; Hermes, *Lib.* V.5, etc.). And conversely, to reach the world of the unembodied one must have cast away "the heavy weight of the body" (*rūpa-garu-bhāram,* Sdhp. 494); Cf. *Phaedrus* 246B, 248D where it is the "weight of forgetfulness and evil" that arrests "the soul's flight", and St. Augustine, *Conf.* XIII.7—"In what terms shall I describe how the huge weight of lustful desires presses down into the deep abyss, and how charity raises us up again by Thy spirit which moved over the waters?"

Otherwise stated, the power of levitation is exercised "by an envelopment of the body in the (tarn-) cloak of contemplation" (*jhāna-veṭhanena sarīram veṭhetvā,* J.V.126; SA.XIV), where the power is at the same time one of dis-appearance. Cf. Comfort, *Chretien de Troyes,* p.193; Dante, *Paradiso* X.74, XXVII.64.

Walking on water has other parallels such as moving along a spider's thread or along sunbeams or flying in the air. Cf. Hesiod, *Catalogue of Women,* 84, *ni-lip* to make vanish Āt to vanish. See also: Cuchullain's *mantle* of immobility; W.N. Brown *Twain,* p. 42; J. Kalingabodi . . . -flight through air, *jhāna veṭhanena.* H.S.V. Jones, "The Cleomades and Related Folk Tales"; "Flying through the air in traditional literature", in *Proceedings of the Modern Languages Association,* Vol. 23, 1908; Dabba's ascension; *Udāna* 93 (rises, 'becomes a flame', body in brief consumed); A.B. Keith, AA.22 on *tapas* and *sati*; A.M. Hocart, "Flying through the Air"; A. Avalon, *Mahanirvāṇa Tantra* CXXVIII—"From *prāṇāyāma* arises *lāghava* (lightness)".

On shape shifting see my "Tanukṛt", Bharat Kaumudi I, 1945.

[129]S.V.25f.; A.I.254; S.II.212; M.I.34 and passim: explanations, Vis. 393f.

[130]Failure follows want of "faith"; or any distraction from contemplation as in J.V.125-7.

[131]RV.IX.86.44; JB.II.34; ŚB.IV.3.4.5; AB.II.39-41; VI.27-31; KU.VI.17, etc.

intellectual body that one enjoys omniscience and is a mover-at-will as far as the Brahmaloka.[132]

Before we ask ourselves what all this means, let us remark that supernatural no more implies unnatural than super-essential implies unessential; and that it would be unscientific to say that such attainments are impossible, unless one has made experiment in accordance with the prescribed and perfectly intelligible disciplines. To call these things "miraculous" is not to say "impossible", but only "wonderful"; and as we said before, following Plato, "Philosophy begins in wonder". Furthermore, it must be clearly understood that the Buddha, like other orthodox teachers, attaches no great importance to these powers and very strongly deprecates a cultivation of powers for their own sake and in any case forbids their public exhibition by monks who possess them. "I do, indeed", he says, "possess these three powers (*ṛddhi*) of motion-at-will, mind-reading, and teaching; but there can be no comparison of the first two of these marvels (*pratihārya*) with the much farther-reaching and far more productive marvel of my teaching".[133] It will profit us more to ask what such marvels, or those of Christ imply, than to ask whether they "really" took place on some given occasion;[134] just as in the exegesis of other hero-tales it

[132]As Śaṅkaracārya explains in connection with Pras.Up.IV.5, it is the *mano-maya ātman* that enjoys omniscience and can be where and as it will. Cf. RV.III.53.8 *māyāḥ kṛṇvānas tanvam pari svām;* BG.VII.25 *nāham prakāśaḥ sarvasya yogamāyā samāvṛtaḥ;* Viṣṇu Purana VI-7-43 *kuryāt cittānu kāriṇipratyāhāra parāyaṇaḥ.* This "intellectual self or body" (*añño attā dibbo rūpī manomayo,* D.I.34, cf. I.77, M.II.17) the Buddha has taught his disciples how to extract from the physical body; and it is clearly in this "other, divine, intellectual body", and not in his human capacity, not at all times or under all conditions "whether in motion or at rest, or sleeping or waking" (*carato ca me tiṭṭhato ca suttassa ca jāgarassa ca*) but "when he will" (*yāvade akaṅkhāmi,* as in the *iddhi* contexts; cf. *Twain,* importance of movability, like 'bark') that the Buddha himself can recall (*anussarāmi*) his own former births, without limit, can survey "with the divine eye, transcending human vision" the births and deaths of other beings, here and in other worlds, over and beyond which he has verified here and now the double liberation (M.I.482). The expression "sleeping or waking" lends itself to a lengthy exegesis. Note that the order of words connects motion with sleep and immobility with waking. This means that as in so many Upanisad contexts, "sleep", that sleep in which one "comes into one's own" (*svapiti = svam apītaḥ bhavati,* CU.VI.8.1, ŚB.X.5.2.14) it is not the sleep of exhaustion, but the "sleep of contemplation" (dhyāna) that is intended; it is precisely in this state of "sleep" in which the senses are withdrawn that there is motion-at-will (*supto . . . prāṇān gṛhītvā sve śarīre yathā-kāmam parivartate,* BU.II.1.18), in this contemplative sleep that "striking down what is physical, the Sunbird, the Immortal, goes where he will" (*dhyāyatīva . . . svapno bhūtvā . . . śarīram abhiprahatyā . . . īyate'mṛto yatra kāmam,* BU.IV.3.7, 11, 12).

[133]A.I.171, 172—Of the three powers, of remembrance of births, reading the thoughts of others, and teaching (*adesa-pāṭi-hāriyam*), the latter is the most considerable and most productive (*abhikkaṅkataraṁ ca paṇitataraṁ ca*).

[134]"No marvel it was that the Water of Life revived the dead fish: The marvel was that the dead fish showed the way to the Fountain of Life". *Sikandar Nāmā,* LXIX. 48-9.

will be much more useful to ask what "seven-league boots" and "tarn caps" mean, than to point out that they cannot be bought in department stores.

In the first place, we observe that in the Brāhmaṇical contexts, omniscience, particularly of births, is predicated of Agni (*jātavedas*), the "Eye in the World", and of the "all-seeing" Sun, the "Eye of the Gods", and for the very good reason that these consubstantial principles are the catalytic powers apart from which no birth could be; and further, that the power of motion at will, or what is the same thing, motion without locomotion, is predicated in the Brāhmaṇical books of the Spirit or Universal Self (*ātman*) on the one hand, and of liberated beings, knowers of the Self and assimilated to the Self, on the other. Once we have understood that the Spirit, universal solar Self and Person, is a timeless omnipresence, it will be recognized that the Spirit, by hypothesis, is naturally possessed of all the powers that have been described; the Spirit is the "knower of all births" *in saecula saeculorum* precisely because it is "where everywhere and every when are focussed" and is present undivided as well in all past as in all future becomings;[135] and by the same token, we find it spoken of also as "Providence (*prajñā*) or as "Compendious Providence" (*prajñāna-ghana*) for the very good reason that its knowledge of "events" is not derived from the events themselves, but the events derived from its knowledge of itself. In all the Brāhmaṇical books the powers that have been described are the Lord's: if the Comprehensor can change his form and move at will, it is "even as Brahma can change his form and move at will;[136] it is the Spirit, ultimately solar Self (*ātman*) that itself not moving yet out runs others.[137] All these things are powers of the Spirit and of those who are "in the spirit"; and if by far the greatest of all these miracles is that of the teaching, that is simply to say with St. Ambrose that "All that is true, by whomsoever it has been said, is from the Holy Ghost".[138] If the "signs and wonders" are lightly dismissed, it is not because they are unreal, but because it is an evil and adulterous generation that asketh for a sign.

The Buddha describes himself as unknowable (*ananuvedya*) even here and now; neither Gods nor men can see him; those who see him in any form or think of him in words do not see him at all.[139] "I am neither priest nor prince nor husbandman nor anyone at all; I wander in the world a learned Nobody, uncontaminate by human qualities (*alipyamāna . . .-mānavebhyah*); useless to ask my family name (gotra)".[140] He leaves no trace by which he can be

[135]AV.X.8.1, 12; KU.IV.13; Praś.Up.IV.5, etc.

[136]ŚA.VII.22.

[137]BU.IV.3.12; Īśā.Up.4; MU.II.2.

[138]St. Ambrose, gloss on I Cor. 12.3.

[139]M.I.140, 141. The Buddha is *ananuvejjo*, "past finding out", similarly other Arahats are traceless (*vaṭṭaṁ tesaṁ n'atthi paññpānāya*). S.I.23; *Vajracchedika Sūtra*; cf. S.III.IIIf., and Hermes *Lib.* XIII.3.

[140]Sn. 455, 456, 648.

"Give up identification with your family, your clan, your name, and station in life which are associated with your living body—". Śaṅkarācārya, *Vivekachudamani*, 298.

tracked.[141] Even here and now the Buddha cannot be taken hold of, and it cannot be said of this Supernal Person (*parama-puruṣa*) after the dissolution of the body and psychic complex that he becomes or does not become, nor can both these things be affirmed or denied of him; all that can be said is that "he is"; to ask what or where he is would be futile.[142] "He who sees the Law (dharma) sees me";[143] and that is why in the early iconography he is represented, not in human form, but by such symbols as that of the "Wheel of the Law", of which he is the immanent mover. And that is all just as it was in the Brāhmaṇical books, where it is Brahma that has no personal or family name[144] and cannot be tracked, the Spirit (*ātman*) that never became anyone—Who knows where he is?[145]—the interior Self that is uncontaminated,[146] the supreme Self of which nothing true can be said (*neti, neti*) and that cannot be grasped except by the thought "It is". It is assuredly with reference to that ineffable principle that the Buddha says that "There is an unborn, unbecome, unmade, incomposite, and were it not for that unborn, unbecome, unmade, incomposite, no way could be shown of escape from birth, becoming, making, composition";[147] and we do not see what that "unborn" can be but "That" inanimate (*anātmya*) Spirit (*ātman*) were it not for whose invisible being (*sat*) there could be no life anywhere.[148] The Buddha flatly denies that he ever taught the cessation or annihilation of an essence; all that he teaches is the putting of a stop to sorrow.[149]

In a famous passage of the Milinda Questions the old symbol of the chariot is used by Nagasena to break down the King's belief in the reality of his own

[141]Dh. 179 (*tam buddham anantagocaram apadaṁ, kena padena nessatha*); like Brahmā, BU.III.8.8, Mund Up.I.2.6; Devas JUB.III.35.7 (*na . . . padam asti, padena ha vai punar mṛtyur anveti*); Gāyatrī, BU.V.14.7 (*apad asi, na hi padyase*, Śaṅkaracārya *netinetyātmavat*). All this has to do with the originally and ultimately footless (ophidian) nature of the Godhead, whose *vestigia pedis* mark the Way only so far as up to the Sundoor, Janua Coeli. Cf. note 139 (Buddhism).

[142]S.III.116f, 118 *tathāgato anupalabbhiyamāno*. Cf. S.V.282f. on *iddhis* of the Tathāgata. *Yasmin samaye Tathāgato kāyam pi citte samādahati* (synthesizes body in mind) *āttam pi kāye samādahat*: and enters into and experiences the sense of bliss and lightness, then the Tathagata's body becomes lighter, more workable, and more radiant . . . and at such time the Tathāgata's body easily (*appa kasirena*) rises up from the earth into the air and he (*abhi ud gacchati*) then enjoys (*paccanubhoti*) all sorts of *iddhis*. . . .

[143]S.III.120 *yo kho dhammam passati mam passati*.

[144]BU.III.8.8; Mund Up.I.1.6; JUB.III.14.1; Rūmī, *Mathnawī* I.3055-65.

[145]KU.II.18, 25; cf. Mil. 73, the Buddha "is", but "neither here nor there"; in the Dhamma-body alone can he be designated. *Parinibbāna* in life, at death or hereafter; at least the streamwinner becomes an *akanitthagāmi*.

[146]BU.IV.4.23; KU.V.11; MU.III.2, etc.

[147]Udāna 80, 93; CU.VIII.13.

[148]Taitt.Up.II.7; cf. note 37 (Buddhism). *Phaedrus* 247C—*achrōmatos te kai aschēmatistos kai anaphēs ousia . . . monō theatē nōl* = colourless and formless, intangible essence . . . visible only to mind (*adeiktos* = not shown).

[149]M.I.137-40, cf. D.II.68 and passim.

"personality".[150] We need hardly say that throughout the Brāhmaṇical and Buddhist literature (as also in Plato and Philo)[151] the "chariot" stands for the psycho-physical vehicle, as which or in which—according to our knowledge of "who we are"—we live and move.[152] The steeds are the senses, the reins their controls, the mind the coachman, and the Spirit or real Self (*ātman*) the charioteer (*rathī*),[153] i.e. passenger and owner, who alone knows the vehicle's destination; if the horses are allowed to run away with the mind, the vehicle will go astray; but if they are curbed and guided by the mind in accordance with its knowledge of the Self, the latter will reach home. In our Buddhist text it is strongly emphasized that all that composes the chariot and team, or body-and-soul, is devoid of any essential substance; "chariot" and "self" are only the conventional names of *constructed* (constituted) aggregates, and do not import existences independent of or distinguishable from the factors of which they are composed; and just as one confection is called a "chariot" for convenience, so ought the human personality to be called a "self" only for convenience. And just as the repeated expression "That is not my Self" has so often been misinterpreted to mean "There is no Self" so the destructive analysis of the vehicular personality has been held to mean that there is no Person! It is complained that "the charioteer is left out".[154]

Actually, however, nothing is said for or against the imperceptible presence in the composite vehicle of an eternal substance distinct from it and one and the same in all such vehicles. Nagasena, who refuses to be regarded as a "somebody" and maintains that "Nagasena" is nothing but a name for the inconstant aggregate of the psycho-physical phenomenon, could surely have

[150]Mil.26-8; S.I.135; Vis.593-4.

[151]Eg. *Laws* 898 Df., *Phaedrus* 246E-256D, cf. note 153 (Buddhism).

[152]"As which" if we identify ourselves with the "personality"; "in which" if we recognize our Self as the Inner Person.

[153]The charioteer is either Agni (RV.X.51.6; AV.III.21.3), or the Breath (*prāṇa* = Brahma, Ātman, Sun), the Breath to which "no name can be given" (AA.II.3.8), or the Spiritual Self (Ātman, KU.III.3; J.V.252) or Dhamma (S.I.33). The skilled charioteer (*susārathi*) guides his horses where he will (RV.VI.75.6),—just as we might now speak of the skilled driver of a motorcar or aeroplane as roaming where he likes.
So Boethius, *De Consolatione Philosophiae*, IV.1

Where the great King his sceptre holds, and the
  World's reins doth guide aright,
And, firm in his swift chariot, doth everything in order set.

Hic regum sceptrum dominus tenet/Orbisque habenas temperat/Et volucrem currum stabilis regit/Rerum coruscus arbiter.

The contrast of good and vicious horses (the senses) in KU.III.6, Dh. 94 and Svet.Up.II.9, cf. RV.X.44.7 parallels Phaedrus 248E.

[154]Mrs. Rhys Davids, *Milinda Questions*, 1930, p. 33. [It must be remembered that Mrs. Rhys Davids was a spiritualist. In answer to her words on the little page of Śākya might be cited Vis. 594 "There are Gods and men who delight in becoming. When they are taught the Law for the cessation of becoming, their mind does not respond"].

said, "I live, yet not 'I', but the Law in me". And if we take into consideration other Pali texts we shall find that a charioteer is taken for granted, and who and what he is, namely one that "has never become anyone". The Eternal Law (*dharma*) is, in fact, the charioteer;[155] and while "the king's chariots age, and just so the body ages, the Eternal Law of existences does not age".[156] The Buddha identifies himself—that Self that he calls his refuge[157]—with this Law[158] and calls himself the best of charioteers",[159] one who tames men, as

[155]S.I.33 *dhammāhaṁ sārathiṁ brūmi.* Cf. Jataka No. 457. *dhammo na jaraṁ upeti;* Sn. 1139 *dhammam . . . sanditthikam akālikam.*

W.M. Urban, *The Intelligible World*, 1929, p. 231—Men "feel that what cannot be put in terms of time is meaningless" . . . ; [But] W.H. Sheldon, in *Modern Schoolman* XXI.133—". . . the notion of a static, immutable being ought to be understood rather as signifying a process so intensely vivacious, in terms of times so extremely swift, as to comprise beginning and end at one stroke". No *individual* can see *all at once.*

"Plus la vie du moi s'identifie avec la vie du non-moi, plus on vil intensemont" Abdul Hadi, "L'Immortalite en Islam", *Voile d'Isis,* January 1934.

Still waters run deep.

[156]D.II.120 *katam me saraṇam attano.*

[157]St. Thomas, *Sum.Theol.* I.11.91 *Filius Dei . . . est ipsa lex aeterna* = "the son of God is that eternal love".

[158]S.III.120 *yo kho dhammam passati so mam passati, yo mam passati so dhammam passati;* so Sn. 934 *sakkhi dhammam . . . adassi.* Similarly D.III.84 *Bhagavato'mhi . . . dhammajo . . . Dhammakāyo iti pi brahmakāyo iti pi, dhamma bhūto iti pi,* S.II.221 *Bhagavato'mhi putto . . . dhammajo;* S.IV.94 *dhammabhūto brahmabhūto . . . dhammasāmi tathāgato:* A.II.211 *brahmabhūtena attanā;* S.III.83 *brahmabhūtā . . . buddhā.* There can be no doubt whatever of the equations *dhamma* = *brahma* = *buddha* = *attā:* as in BU.II.5.11 *ayam dharmaḥ . . . ayam ātmā idam amṛtam idaṁ brahma idaṃ sarvam.* In Dh. 169, 364, (II.25.2) *dhamma* is clearly the equivalent of *brahma, ātman.* A Buddha is whatever all or any of these terms denote, and by the same token "not any what" (*akiṁcano,* Dh. 421, Sn. 1063), and "without analogy" (*yassa n'atthi upamā kvaci,* Sn. 1139).

Cf. *Śaiva Siddhānta Samgraha* IV.5 for the identity of *Brahman* and *ātman.*

M.I.111 *Bhagavā jānam jānāti, passam passati, cakkhubhūto, ñānabhūto, dhammabhūto, brahmabhūto.*

"Buddha is the Knower of knowing, Seer of seeing, is become the Eye, become the Gnosis, become the Dhamma, Brahma-become". That Buddha is identified with Brahma, is also implied by *yakkha.* See *yakṣa* of the Ṛgveda and the Upanisads. "That which the Buddha preached, the Dhamma *kat'exochen* (distinction, excellence), was the order of law of the universe, immanent, eternal, uncreated, not as interpreted by him only, much less invented or decreed by him" (PTS. Pali Dictionary, see Dhamma).

[159]Sn. 83 *buddhaṁ dhammasāminaṁ vītataṇhaṁ dīpaduttamaṁ sārathīnam pavaram. Dhammasāmi* = RV.X.129.3 *satyadharmendra,* RV.X.129.3, 8, 9 "the one King of the world, God of Gods, Satyadharmā". Cf. RV.I.12.7, X.34.8; and the *dhārmas-tejomayo' mṛtamayaḥ puruṣaḥ . . . ayamātmā . . . idam brahma* of BU.II.5.11. The Buddhist Dhamma (*nomos, logos,* ratio) is the eternal Dharma of BU.I.5.23 ("him, Vāyu, Prāṇa, the Gods made their Law"); and BU.I.4.14 "There is nothing beyond this Law, this Truth"; Sn. 884 "The Truth is one, indeed, there is no other".

though they were horses.[160] And finally we find a detailed analysis of the "chariot" concluding with the statement that the rider is the Self (*ātman*), in almost the very words of the Upanishads.[161] The statement of a Buddhist commentator, that the Buddha is the Spiritual Self (*ātman*) is assuredly correct.[162] That "Great Person" (*mahāpuruṣa*) is the charioteer in all beings.

We believe that enough has now been said to show beyond any possible doubt that the "Buddha" and "Great Person", "Arhat", "Brahma-become" and "God of Gods" of the Pali texts is himself the Spirit (*ātman*) and Inner Man of all beings, and that he is "That One" who makes himself manifold in whom all beings again "become one"; that the Buddha is Brahma, Prajāpati, the Light of Lights, Fire or Sun, or by whatever other name the older books refer to the First Principle; and to show that in so far as the Buddha's "life" and deeds are described, it is the doings of Brahma as Agni and Indra that are retold. Agni and Indra are the Priest and King *in divinis*, and it is with these two possibilities that the Buddha is born, and these two possibilities that are realised, for although his kingdom is in one sense not of this world, it is equally certain that he as Cakravartin is both priest and king in the same sense that Christ is "both priest and king". We are forced by the logic of the scriptures[163] themselves to say that Agnendrau, Buddha, Krishna, Moses and Christ are names of one and the same "descent" whose birth is eternal; to recognize that all scripture without exception requires of us in positive terms to know our Self and by the same token to know what-is-not-our-Self but mistakenly called a "self "; and that the Way to become what-we-are demands an excision from our consciousness-of-being, every false identification of our being with what-we-are-not, but think we are when we say "I think" or "I do". To have "come clean" (*śuddha, katharos*) is to have distinguished our Self from all its psycho-physical, bodily and mental accidents; to have identified our Self with any of these is the worst possible sort of pathetic fallacy and the whole cause of "our" sufferings and mortality, from which no one who still is anyone can be liberated. It is related that a Confucian scholar be sought the twenty-eighth Buddhist patriarch, Bodhidharma, "to pacify his soul". The Patriarch retorted, "Produce it, and I will pacify it". The Confucian replied "That is my

---

M.II.206-7: What Buddha teaches is *brahmāṇam* "the way to fellowship with Brahman" [*sahavyatāya maggo* (*sahāya* = *saha+aya*); A.5.90 *kalyāṇa-sahāyo*, Manusmṛti VI.49 *ātmanaiva sahāyena*], and can teach because he can say *brahmāṇam caham . . . brahma lokam prajānāmi*, as being one who was "born there and had always lived there". Cf. BG.XVIII.54 *brahma-bhūta prasannātmā.*

[160]Vin.I.35, A.I.173, II.155.

[161]J.VI.252 *kāyo te ratha . . . attā vā sārathi;* S.IV.292 *ratho tikho immass'etam cātumahābhūtikassa kāyassa adhivacanam;* like KU.III.3 *ātmānaṁ rathinaṁ viddhi śarīram rathameva tu. Theragatha* I.574 *Kammayantena rathito*; BG.XVIII.61, Maitri Up.IV.4. Cf. Plato, *Laws* 898C and *Timaeus* 49E *ochēma,* body as vehicle of head, the most divine and ruling part.

[162] *Udāna* 67 Commentary.

[163]Cf. Sister Nivedita, *The Web of Indian Life,* Ch. XIII.

trouble, that I cannot find it". Bodhidharma replied, "Your wish is granted". The Confucian understood, and departed in peace.[164]

It is altogether contrary to Buddhist, as it is to Vedantic doctrine to think of "ourselves" as wanderers in the fatally determined storm of the world's flow (*saṁsāra*). "Our immortal Self" is anything but a "surviving personality".[165] It is not this man So-and-so that goes home and is lost to view,[166] but the prodigal Self that recollects itself; and that having been many is now again one, and inscrutable, *Deus absconditus.* "No man hath ascended up to heaven, but he that came down from heaven", and therefore "If any man would follow me, let him deny himself".[167] "The kingdom of God is for none but the thoroughly dead".[168] The realisation of Nirvāṇa is the "Flight of the Alone to the Alone".[169] "Tis the Void that passeth to the Void".[170]

NOTE

The foregoing notes and references are far from exhaustive. They are intended to assist the reader to build up a meaning content for several terms that could not be fully explained in the lectures as delivered, and to enable the scholar to follow up some of the sources. In the lectures, Pali words are given in their Sanskrit forms, but in the Notes the Pali is quoted as such. I have taken pains to collate the Buddhist and Brahmanical sources throughout: it might have been even better to treat the whole subject as one, making no distinction of Buddhism from Brahmanism. Indeed, the time is coming when a Summa of the Philosophia Perennis will have to be written, impartially based on all orthodox sources whatever. [This hope expressed by Coomaraswamy was fulfilled in admirable measure by Whitall N. Perry with his: *A Treasury of Tradition Wisdom,* published in 1971.—Ed.]

Some notable Platonic and Christian parallels have been cited (1) in order to bring out more clearly, because in more familiar contexts, the meaning of certain Indian doctrines and (2) to emphasize that the Philosophia Perennis, Sanātana Dharma,

[164] D.T. Suzuki in *Journal of the Pali Text Society,* 1906/7, p. 13.

[165] S.III.25, 26 *yoyam āyasmā evaṁnāmo evaṁgotta = bhārahāro = puggala.*

[166] Sn.1074-6 *nāmakāyā vimutto, attham paleti, na upeti saṅkham . . . atthaṁ gatassa na pamāṇam atthi.*

Mund.Up.III.2.8, 9 *nāmarūpād vimuktaḥ . . . amṛto bhavati;* BG.XV.5 *dvandvair vimuktāḥ.*

[167] John XIII.36; Mark VIII.34. Whoever would follow must be able to say with St. Paul, "I live, yet not *I,* but Christ in me". Gal.II.20. Also von Hildebrandt, *Literature and Personality,* p. 32. There can be no return to God but as of like to like, and that likening, in the words of Cusa, demands an *ablatio omnis alteritatis et diversitatis* (the removal of all altereity and diversity).

[168] Meister Eckhart, Evans edn., I, p. 419.

[169] Plotinus, *Enneads* VI.9.11.

[170] AA.II.3.8 *Yad akṣarād akṣaram eti. Lallā* (Temple, Camb., 1924) p. 184. "Then shalt thou behold of All the sum:—tis the void that passes the void;" and *Lallā-Vākyāni* by Grievson and Barnett (Royal Asia Soc., 1920), p. 33 "shōnēs shūnāh mīlith gano (= "and a void became merged within the void").

Akāliko Dhammo, is always and everywhere consistent with itself. These citations are not made as a contribution to literary history (cf. René Guénon, *Introduction to the Study of the Hindu Doctrines,* 1945, p. 58); we do not suggest that borrowings of doctrines or symbols have been made in either direction, nor that there has been an independent origination of similar ideas, but that there is a common inheritance from a time long antedating our texts, of what St. Augustine calls the "wisdom that was not made, but is at this present, as it hath ever been, and so shall ever be" (*Confessions* IX.10). As Lord Chalmers truly says of the parallels between Christianity and Buddhism, "there is here no question of one creed borrowing from the other; the relationship goes deeper than that" (*Buddha's Teachings,* HOS.37, 1932, p. xx).

The following abbrevaitions are employed:

RV., *Ṛg Veda Saṁhitā,* TS, *Taittiriya Saṁhitā* (Black Yajur Veda); A.V., *Atharva Veda Saṁhitā;* TB., PB., ŚB., AB., KB., JB., JUB., the *Brāhmaṇas,* respectively the *Taittiriya, Pañcaviṁśa, Śatapatha, Aitareya, Kauṣītaki, Jaiminiya, Jaiminiya Upaniṣad;* AA., TA., ŚA., the *Āraṇyakas,* respectively the *Aitareya, Taittirīya* and *Śāṅkhāyana;* BU., CU., TU., Ait., KU., MU., Praś., Muṇḍ., Īśā., the *Upaniṣads,* respectively the *Bṛhadāraṇyaka, Chāndogya, Taittirīya, Aitareya, Kaṭha, Maitri, Praśna, Muṇḍaka* and *Īśāvāsya;* BD., *Bṛhad Devatā;* BG., *Bhagavad Gītā;* Vin., *Vinaya Piṭaka;* A., M., S., the *Nikāyas,* respectively the *Anguttara, Majjhima* and *Saṁyutta;* Sn., *Sutta Nipāta;* DA., *Sumaṅgala Vilāsinī;* Dh., *Dhammapada;* Dh.A., *Dhammapada Atthakathā;* Itiv., *Itivuttaka;* Vis., *Visuddhi Magga;* Mil., *Milinda Pañho;* BC., *Buddhacarita;* HJAS., *Harvard Journal of Asiatic Studies;* JAOS., *Journal of the American Oriental Society;* NIA., *New Indian Antiquary;* IHQ., *Indian Historical Quarterly;* SBB., *Sacred Books of the Buddhists;* HOS., *Harvard Oriental Series.*

Uttiṣṭha jāgrata prāpya varān nibodhata (KU.III.14)
Ye suttā te pabbujjatha (Itiv., p. 41)

INDEX